D1361603

A HISTORY OF NOTTINGHAMSHIRE

Newark Castle

0 1191 0259870 1

DISCARDED

THE DARWEN COUNTY HISTORY SERIES

A History of Nottinghamshire

DAVID KAYE

Drawings by Keith Woodcock

Cartography by R. Fry and M. Church

PHILLIMORE

1987

Published by
PHILLIMORE & CO. LTD.
Shopwyke Hall, Chichester, Sussex

© David Kaye, 1987

ISBN 0 85033 602 3

Printed in Great Britain by
The University Press, Oxford

Contents

Raleigh Works, Nottingham

5

List of Plates

Creswell blade

7

Acknowledgements

The author is most grateful to the following for permission to reproduce photographs: Frank Rodgers (nos. 1, 5, 7, 9-12 inclusive, 14-17 inclusive, 21, 23-25 inclusive, 27, 31, 32 and 41); Philip Harris (nos. 18a and b); Nottinghamshire County Council Leisure Services Department (nos. 22, 26, 28, 34-6 inclusive, 48; and the Nottingham lace advertisement); Graham Beaumont (no. 29); Edward Sturge (no. 33a); John Samuels (no. 33b); and the Trustees of the National Portrait Gallery (nos. 42 and 43).

List of Maps

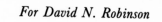

For David N. Robinson

Preface

During the past 20 years I have come to know our neighbouring county of Nottinghamshire very well. I have attended numerous part-time courses at its university; our family have frequently toured its city, and not merely on shopping expeditions; and old friends in Ravenshead have caused us to make regular visits to the county. When I undertook this commission, I welcomed the opportunity to continue and extend my research into Nottinghamshire's history, and to discover in what ways it runs parallel with that of Lincolnshire, where I live, and in what ways it is very different.

In addition to documentary research, much enjoyable fieldwork has included visits to most Nottinghamshire towns and villages, where I have explored, made copious notes and taken hundreds of photographs. It has also been traumatic, for on one occasion my vehicle caught fire in Gotham's market place and burnt out. Like the famous historian of the French Revolution, Thomas Carlyle, before me, I lost all my accumulated notes in the blaze and had to begin again at square one!

Every historian reveals in his text his own favourite aspects of the subject, and I make no apology that my abiding fascination with cricket, politics and public transport has meant that all make strong contributions to this volume.

I owe gratitude to many people. To my long standing friends David Robinson, Jeffrey May and Professor Kenneth Cameron for their specialist knowledge that has enabled me to tackle chapters I, II and IV with reasonable confidence. To Dr. John Samuels who read through my first draft, making useful suggestions for additions and amendments. To Dorothy Ritchie of the Nottingham Local Studies Library, for helping me with suitable old prints and photographs to illustrate my text. To G. L. Roberts and Eric H. Smith, who physically reproduced these, and prints from my own films, so professionally. To Keith Woodcock, Mike Church and Rodney Fry, who were sometimes given almost impossible instructions for converting my photographs and rough plans into marginal drawings and explanatory maps respectively. Finally, to Michael Honeybone and Dr. Frances Condick who kept me going with encouragement when I felt like abandoning the whole project.

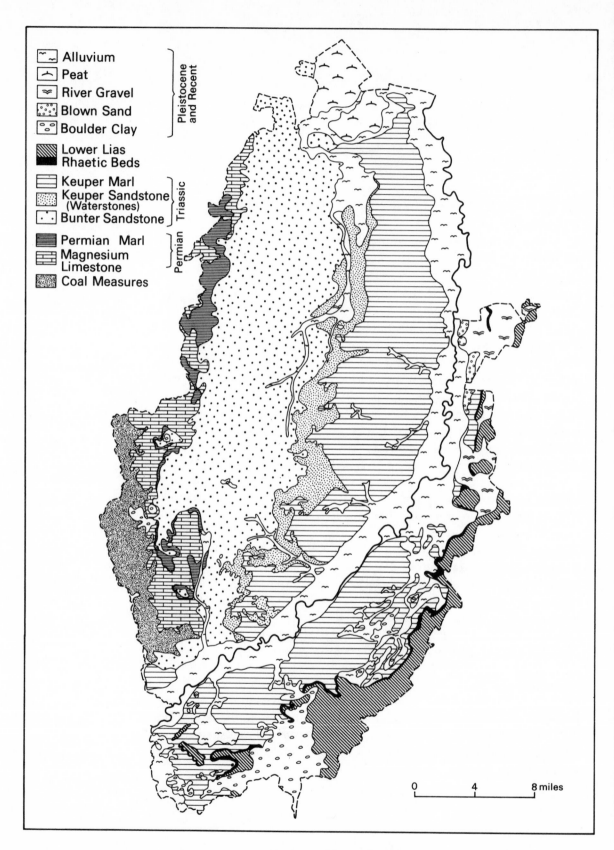

	Alluvium	
	Peat	Pleistocene and Recent
	River Gravel	
	Blown Sand	
	Boulder Clay	
	Lower Lias Rhaetic Beds	
	Keuper Marl	
	Keuper Sandstone (Waterstones)	Triassic
	Bunter Sandstone	
	Permian Marl	
	Magnesium Limestone	Permian
	Coal Measures	

0   4   8 miles

Map 1. The Geology of Nottinghamshire.

I The Setting

Nottinghamshire covers 844 square miles, with its longest, north-south axis 52 miles long. This East Midland county is located between Lowland England to its south and east with its accent on arable agriculture, and the Pennines to the north-west. Its principal physical feature is the north-south domination of its geology.

Through the centre of this county for more than fifty miles flows the broad River Trent with a flood plain that is more than two miles wide in places. This is the main artery for the drainage of most of Nottinghamshire. For centuries the Trent was accounted the boundary of the two halves of England, when, for example, the administration of the royal forests was divided between 'This Side Trent' and 'Yon Side Trent'.

Although in modern times Nottinghamshire has been thought of increasingly in terms of coal production, in fact the Middle Coal Measures occupy only about thirty-five square miles: much less than in neighbouring Derbyshire.

The most westerly geological formation is that of the Permian Magnesium limestone which provides excellent greyish building stone in the Mansfield area, and which once supplied the stone used in the rebuilding of the Houses of Parliament 150 years ago. At the southern end of this escarpment at Bulwell the stone is yellow-brown and of poorer quality.

Next comes the Triassic Bunter sandstone, laid down originally in desert conditions, which is acidic. It is made up of reddish-buff-coloured coarse-grained material, forming a plateau which stretches 36 miles from Bawtry in the north to Nottingham itself in the south. It is between six and eight miles broad and covers more than a quarter of the county. In places these beds are up to 400 feet thick and lie on top of impervious beds of Permian marl. Being porous, these rocks act as natural reservoirs, absorbing up to twenty-three per cent of their own volume in water. It is on this sandstone that Sherwood Forest established itself, with oaks and birches, shrubs and bracken. At Nottingham the Bunter sandstone forms a high bluff overlooking the Trent valley, an ideal site for a castle. A curious local feature is the 25-foot high wind-weathered Hemlock

Stone, to be found along the road which links Bramcote with the A52 to the south-west of the city.

The Keuper Marls cover 40 per cent of Nottinghamshire and form bluffs on either side of the flood plain of the Trent, stretching from Gringley-on-the-Hill in the north to the outskirts of Nottingham. These were laid down in flash flood conditions, followed by evaporation, leaving a semi-arid landscape. It is from these beds that the extensive brick manufacturing industry was established in so many local villages. These beds also yield gypsum from sites around Hawton to the south of Newark. A tougher variety known as Keuper waterstones has a greater sand content. In places the Keuper beds are up to 700 feet (213 m) thick. Through them run narrow ravines known locally as 'dumbles' (e.g. Halloughton Dumble, Lambley Dumble), some of which are up to 30 feet deep.

The form of the middle Trent valley was moulded during two glacial periods of the Ice Age. The trench-like valley contains discontinuous gravel terraces, such as those on the south bank at Holme Pierrepont and Hoveringham, and those on the north bank at Attenborough and Beeston. These fluvial deposits along the Trent are mirrored by others along the valleys of its tributaries the Devon, Idle and Smite. The original course of the Trent flowed eastwards towards the Wash through Ancaster Gap. In the latter stages of the Penultimate Glaciation decaying bulks of ice diverted the Trent basically into its present course to join first the Idle and then the Yorkshire Ouse to form the Humber estuary. The Trent descends only 76 feet during its course through the county – a very gentle gradient of just over one foot per mile.

The Rhaetic beds of dark shales with thin and discontinuous strata of limestone give a narrow escarpment. The cover of glacial Boulder clay is largely limited to the south of the county around Willoughby-on-the-Wolds, and includes small pockets of sand and gravel. Some of it is chalky and contains many flints.

In the north of the county bordering on the Isle of Axholme are found carrs (the local name for drained fenland). These are below high tide level, and needed draining before they could be used for agriculture. Indeed, considerable areas of Nottinghamshire are low lying, 40 per cent of the county being less than 100 feet above sea level. In contrast a mere two per cent of the land exceeds 600 feet as it does at Robin Hood Hills.

Of the other rivers within the county boundaries, the Soar and Erewash (which are shared with neighbouring Leicestershire and Derbyshire respectively), join the Trent near the point where that principal river enters Nottinghamshire. The rivers which drain the Bunter sandstone and become tributaries of the Idle – the Maun, Meden and Poulter – are so diminutive because much of their water is absorbed by the porous sandstone itself.

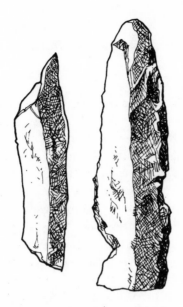

Two examples of Creswell points

II Prehistoric Nottinghamshire

Creswell Crags, one of the most important Palaeolithic sites in Britain, lies astride the modern county boundary between Derbyshire and Nottinghamshire. Of the five major caves on this site Church Hole and Boat House are situated on the Nottinghamshire side of the border. Just before the last great glaciation *c.*43,000 B.C. Neanderthal Man arrived here, at a time when Creswell Crags was also the home of bears, bison, cave lions, wolves and woolly rhinoceroses, all of whose bones were discovered in the 1870s by the Rev. Magens Mello. Church Hole itself penetrates to a distance of 170 feet into the hillside at this point. Amongst other finds in this cave were Lower Palaeolithic axes and scrapers, fashioned by Neanderthals from quartzite, before the advancing ice sheets drove them south. When these glaciers retreated Homo Sapiens moved into Creswell Crags with more sophisticated tools such as points, blades and laurel leaf points. Again, after *c.*25,000 B.C. these caves were left by man for a further period estimated at up to fifteen millennia. Then a group, known to modern archaeologists as Creswellian Man, took up residence. They appear to have hunted wild horses for their meat supply. Indeed the horse appears in art form as well, as in a finely carved horse's head made out of bone. These people also etched abstract patterns on other bones. This raw material provided them with awls and needles, suggesting that they made clothes for themselves. However, like their predecessors, they used flint to make other tools such as their distinctive so-called Creswell points – thin, elongated sharp implements.

Mousterian culture tools made from local quartzite (which occurs naturally in the form of pebbles) have been recovered from the Trent valley at Attenborough. However, some years ago H. H. Swinnerton issued a warning about the provenance of such artifacts, pointing out that the earliest finds may have been carried down by glaciation into south Nottinghamshire, where crude pre-Acheulian tools have been discovered in high level gravels at Beeston, along with later Acheulian artifacts at Cropwell Bishop. Another, Upper Palaeolithic, site has been revealed at Langwith on the banks of the diminutive River Poulter,

Creswell Crags bone needle

16

where a cave yielded finds from the Aurignacian and Magdalenian cultures.

Mesolithic sites are elusive. However, some groups of microlithic tools from this period have been found and sites investigated at Misterton and Tuxford.

We know more about the Neolithic with its fine polished axeheads. A fluted version was found at Wollaton, whilst polished axeheads have been recovered from widely separated sites such as Averham, Beeston, Car Colston, Collingham, Thrumpton and many more along the Trent valley. In 1967 one excellent specimen was rescued from a conveyor belt at a Hoveringham quarry at Holme Pierrepont. This particular axehead has been traced from its origin at Craig Lwyd in North Wales. It was almost 27 cm long and appeared to be in mint condition, having been dropped into the prehistoric Trent before it could be properly fashioned into a suitable tool or weapon. Flint arrowheads dating from the Neolithic period have a widespread distribution, some of them having been found at Gunthorpe, Newark, Tuxford and other sites, often along the banks of the Trent. One drilled stone axehead was dredged from the bed of the river at Barton-in-Fabis. Three unused Group VI (Great Langdale, Cumbria) axeheads were also found in the Trent at Netherfield.

Decorated bone from Creswell Crags

The Bronze Age has yielded up hoards of artifacts such as the one found during building operations in Great Freeman Street in Nottingham in 1860. This hoard included 16 socketed axeheads, four socketed spearheads and a palstave. Another find at Newark consisted of socketed axeheads, two perforated bronze discs and a broad socketed spearhead. An Early Bronze Age thin butted flat axe has been unearthed in more recent times at Mansfield Woodhouse. A Middle Bronze Age unlooped palstave at Gotham was found, and this village has also yielded to archaeologists a Late Bronze Age socketed axe, bringing the grand total of such finds in this county to around eighty. The Trent was used as an important artery for both travel and trade, as riverine settlements such as that found at Clifton, opposite the future site of Nottingham, indicate.

A tri-horned bronze bull's head found on the Roman site of Ad Pontem (see following chapter) seems to be a model of a Celtic deity. Religious beliefs of this period were often reflected in burial customs and rites. Two hundred years ago two socketed axeheads were recovered at Coombes (near Southwell) in association with a possible cremation. Recently a large cemetery dating from the Bronze Age has been excavated at Coneyfor Farm, Hoveringham.

It was probably in either the Late Bronze Age or in the Iron Age that many of the so-called hill forts were constructed in Britain. These

Axe head from Wollaton

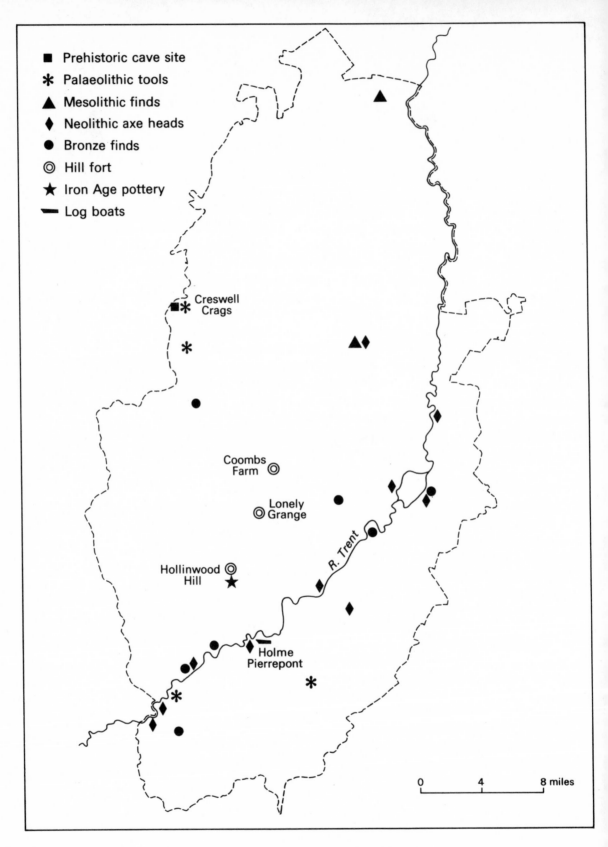

Legend:

■ Prehistoric cave site
✳ Palaeolithic tools
▲ Mesolithic finds
♦ Neolithic axe heads
● Bronze finds
◎ Hill fort
★ Iron Age pottery
▬ Log boats

Creswell Crags

Coombs Farm

Lonely Grange

Hollinwood Hill

R. Trent

Holme Pierrepont

0   4   8 miles

Map 2. Prehistoric Nottinghamshire.

needed careful planning and a degree of social organisation and cohesion that was probably lacking before that period. It is from this era, too, that the considerable network of green lanes and ridgeways dates, which for many centuries provided highways for travellers, ways like Leeming Lane near Mansfield. Often both these man-made features are found close to one another, as at Coombs Farm Camp at Farnsfield. This is an irregular eliptical earthwork enclosing approximately three acres, and overlooks Stone Street – an ancient trackway that linked the future sites of Bawtry and Nottingham. However, some of the forts to the north of the Trent may well date from the Late Bronze Age rather than from the Iron Age. What cannot be verified without scientific archaeological excavation is whether these forts are even earlier and lie on top of Neolithic causewayed camps, as has been proved at Cissbury Ring in West Sussex, for instance. As Professor Barry Cunliffe has pointed out, although we call them 'forts', in fact they probably had other more important everyday functions, such as assembly points. The fact that the Danes adapted Yarborough Camp in South Humberside for their local wapentake meet is an indication that this may have happened elsewhere in the East Midlands. Of the Nottinghamshire forts, Lonely Grange near Oxton is rectangular with axes of 942 feet and 201 feet. Another and much larger camp of this shape was on Hollinwood Hill, Arnold, with axes of 1,251 feet and 720 feet.

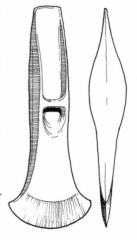

Winged celt from Colwick

Excavations at Ramsdale Park, Arnold, in 1974 revealed Iron Age pottery dating to pre-50 B.C. These pots were hand-made not wheel produced. However, comparatively little pottery has so far been unearthed from this section of the Trent valley.

By the first century B.C. Britain had been divided into 16 separate tribal states. Each of these had one or more *oppidum* or tribal capital, of which Leicester (the future Roman town of *Ratae*) was the centre for the *Coritani* (or *Corieltauvi*). Their territory included the present county of Nottinghamshire and stretched over much of what is now Lincolnshire too. John Wacher believes that sometime before the Roman occupation began the *Coritani* had come under the aegis of the *Belgae*, who controlled most of south-east Britain. There was, for instance, a long common frontier with the powerful Belgic tribe called the *Catuvellauni*, whose main base was in Hertfordshire. The *Coritani* issued their own coinage, and coin moulds have been discovered at both Leicester and at Old Sleaford in Lincolnshire.

The Trent continued, along with its important tributary the Soar, to be vital for the *Coritani* – as it had been for countless generations before. In 1967 at Holme Pierrepont three log boats were uncovered in a quarry, where they had been left high and dry when the river course changed sometime in the Iron Age. Carbon 14 dating suggests that they were made out of trees that were growing sometime between 445 B.C. and 115 B.C.

Bronze socketed spear-head from Gringley

III Roman Nottinghamshire

In A.D. 43 the Emperor Claudius invaded Britain. Within four years the majority of the lowland zone of Britain had been subdued, including the territory of the *Coritani*.

By A.D. 47 the Fosse Way had been built by the Governor Aulus Plautius, stretching from the future town of *Lindum Colonia* (Lincoln) to *Isca Dumnoniorum* (Exeter). As Professor S. S. Frere has pointed out, this major highway, marking as it does the temporary frontier of the embryonic province of *Britannia*, never deviates more than six miles from its alignment over its total distance of 220 miles. To the west of Fosse Way were planted some early, temporary military posts at Broxtowe, Farnsfield and other sites. The Romans placed posting stations at fairly regular intervals along Fosse Way, and four of these were in the future county of Nottinghamshire. The first was 12 miles out of Lincoln at *Crococolana* (the modern hamlet of Brough, near Newark). Coin evidence indicates that it was occupied until the close of the fourth century. However, excavations carried out by Malcolm Dean in the 1960s showed no traces of pottery prior to the beginning of the second century. Next came *Ad Pontem* (near East Stoke to the south of Newark, but actually within the parish of Thorpe). Here John Wacher found structural evidence of a fort, which was probably about two acres in area.

A further six miles brought the Roman traveller to the largest of these stations by far, that of *Margidunum* (Castle Hill, East Bridgford), at the junction of the Fosse Way (the present A46) and Bridgford Street (alias Newton Street, the A6097). This was rhomboid in shape and may have covered up to eight acres. Before work began on the present roundabout at this ancient junction Malcolm Todd was able to excavate part of the site in 1966-8. Both then and in the earlier excavations of Adrian Oswald enormous quantities of Claudio-Neronian and Flavian pottery were found, suggesting that this small town (for that is what it became) was founded *c*.A.D. 50. Margidunum's defences were begun in the late second century with a rampart some 25 feet wide and at least one accompanying ditch. This was made up of bands of dark soil, clay and turf. Later a second rampart was constructed in front of the first one, making the whole 30 feet in width. At one time there were two six-foot ditches dug into the thick Keuper Marl. The innermost of these was approximately 9½ feet wide and the outer 18 feet across. Fragmentary remains of a later wall were also uncovered, the base of which was probably some nine feet wide. It had a compact core of herringbone pitching set into hard white mortar. This wall had apparently been faced with blocks of oolitic limestone transported from Lincolnshire and was probably completed by the late third or fourth century. One rectangular building which was excavated measured 12 feet by 24 feet, and had been divided into two rooms. Local skerry stone had been extracted from the Keuper Marl beds and used in constructing some buildings, the earliest of such dating from c.150. After the military occupation of the site ended c.75 the official staff at *Margidunum* may have included a *beneficiarius consularis*, who was probably of centurion rank and was responsible for security and the collection of road tolls. The whole site may have been occupied after the end of Roman rule since outside the southern defences was a late inhumation cemetery containing some Saxon material.

A further 13 miles on and almost into the future Leicestershire was *Vernemetum* (Willoughby-on-the-Wolds). Excavations here in 1947/8 revealed no pottery earlier than the beginning of the second century.

The other principal Roman road in the county was a branch off Ermine Street, known today as Tillbridge Lane. This forked westwards from the main *Londinium* (London) to *Eboracum* (York) highway a few miles north of *Lindum Colonia* (by the site of the present Lincolnshire Showground). It entered Nottinghamshire after crossing the Trent on what was possibly a pontoon bridge, for fragments of suitable timbering have been dredged from the river at this point. It passed through the posting station of *Segelocum* (Littleborough), before proceeding across country towards *Danum* (Doncaster) and so on to *Eboracum* – an alternative to the crossing of the Humber (*Abus Flumen*) by ferry from Winteringham to *Petvaria* (Brough-on-Humber). Another possible Roman road, later referred to as Leming Lane, connected the future sites of Mansfield and Worksop.

Roman villa sites have been located at Aslockton, Barton-in-Fabis, Car Colston, Cromwell, Epperstone, Lockington, Mansfield Wood-house, Ratcliffe-on-Soar, Southwell and Styrrup. Part of the mosaic and wall plaster from the Southwell villa can be seen inside Southwell Minster. Some villas were situated near known Roman roads (e.g. Mansfield Woodhouse near Leming Lane; Styrrup near Tillbridge Lane). The Mansfield Woodhouse complex was excavated by Major Rooke (whose name is immortalised in the Major Oak in Sherwood) in 1786 and re-excavated by Adrian Oswald 150 years later. The main

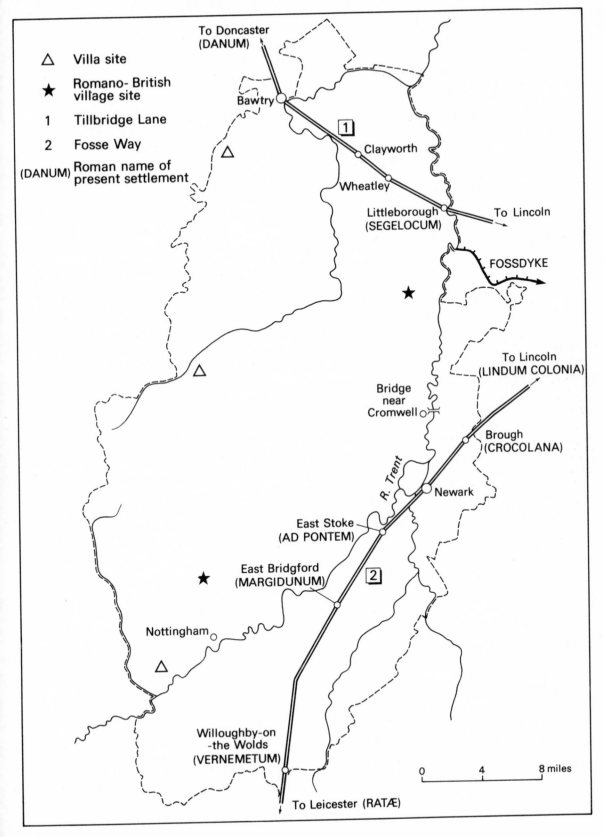

Map 3. Roman Nottinghamshire.

buildings covered an area measuring 142 feet by 40 feet, and contained rooms with painted wall plaster. A second, but smaller, group of buildings on this site had mosaic floors and wall plaster painted in purple, red, yellow and green stripes. E. Greenfield's excavations on Red Hill, Ratcliffe-on-Soar, in 1963 revealed that a Romano-British temple had been situated nearby, suggesting that this may have been near an early fording point on the Trent. Amongst the finds here were two lead tablets on which were scratched curses.

At Broxtowe and Tuxford Romano-British farmsteads have been found with sunken-floor huts; in northern Nottinghamshire Derrick Riley has examined, from the air, crop markings which are indicative of Romano-British field systems.

Lead pigs from the thriving mines in neighbouring Derbyshire have been recovered from the county, evidence of trade from there via the Trent (*Trisante Flumen*) into the Humber. Pottery must also have come into Nottinghamshire in Roman times since no kiln sites like those discovered in Lincolnshire, Yorkshire and along the banks of the Nene at Caister (near Peterborough) have so far been uncovered, apart from one possible such site in Newark.

Roman altar

The dedications of Bole and Saundby churches to St Martin (the early bishop of Tours, who had previously served in the Roman legions) can be taken as evidence for the use of the Trent, if similar evidence from Lincolnshire is taken into consideration. The Romans must have expended enormous effort in digging the Fossdyke, the canal that linked the Trent near Torksey with *Lindum Lolonia* and the river Witham. John Wacher has postulated that its construction may have taken place in the reign of the Emperor Hadrian (117-138). Downstream from *Lindum Colonia* another Roman canal, the Car Dyke, ran along the edge of the grain-growing fens to a point near Cambridge, thus giving the whole Trent valley access to this rich food supply.

1. (*right*) Stapleford's Saxon cross in St Helen's churchyard is the most important pre-Conquest monument in Nottinghamshire and is thought to date from *c*.1050.

2. (*below*) Part of the remains of Mattersey Priory of the Gilbertian Order on the banks of the River Idle.

3. (*left*) St Helen's church at South Wheatley has been a ruin since 1883. Amongst its few remains is the Norman chancel arch.

4. (*below*) When the church of St Mary and All Saints, Hawksworth, was rebuilt in 1851, this primitively carved tympanum was retained.

5. (*above*) Worksop's Cluniac priory gatehouse is a 14th-century structure with a later oriel window.

6. (*right*) This preaching cross, at Gringley-on-the-Hill, stands on the edge of the hills that slope down to the valley of the Idle.

7. (*left*) St Mary's church, Edwinstowe, is an early medieval structure. A Saxon shrine to St Edwin stood somewhere in this area.

8. (*below*) St Swithin's church at East Retford was almost rebuilt in 1855, its Early English central tower having collapsed in 1651.

IV   Mercia and the Danelaw

An exact date for the displacement of Roman *Britannia* by Anglo-Saxon England does not exist, for it was a very gradual transition. Archaeologists are still finding clues as to its nature, but it will be many years before anything like a complete picture emerges. Some form of life may have continued on the villa sites for an undefined length of time, whilst those who lived in the Romano-British settlements and farmsteads must have continued their lives much as before and, since Nottinghamshire is some way from the sea, this pattern would have persisted here for longer than in some of the coastal regions. However, during the latter half of the fifth century an increasing number of immigrants from north-west Europe crossed the North Sea and began of a new life in Britain.

By the beginning of the seventh century most of what was to become England had been colonised and seven independent, warring kingdoms had been established. These are known to historians collectively as the Heptarchy, and their unofficial leader was called the Bretwalda. Four of these kingdoms were smaller than the others, three of them being swallowed up by their more powerful neighbours at an early date (Essex, Kent and Sussex), although that of East Anglia continued until it was overrun by the Danes in 870. The Angles, the tribe who conquered the East Midlands, founded the Kingdom of Mercia (a name meaning 'boundary folk'), which had its capital in the Tamworth area of Staffordshire. Although Mercia's boundaries were rather fluid, the Trent appeared to form its eastern limits for much of its history. Beyond this natural barrier lay the short-lived kingdom of Lindsey – a zone which was desired by both Mercia and its powerful northern rival, the kingdom of Northumbria, which between 617 and 633 was led by the strong King Edwin, who had made himself ruler by defeating his predecessor King Athelferth on the banks of the River Idle at the northernmost extremity of Nottinghamshire. Having married the Christian daughter of the King of Kent, Edwin and his court are said to have been baptised in 627 in the waters of the Trent at a place chronicled as 'Tiorulfingacestir'. The final element in this place-name is a corruption of the Latin word *Castra*, meaning a camp (i.e. a Roman fort or small town). It is said by some authorities that this refers to *Segolocum* (the present Littleborough). By this time Edwin was accepted (albeit reluctantly) by his peers as Bretwalda. But already this title was threatened by an unholy alliance of King Penda of Mercia and his Welsh ally Cadwallan. On 14 October 633 the forces of Mercia and Northumbria met at Hatfield Chase, where in the ensuing battle Edwin was amongst the slain. The exact location of this bloody conflict is not known, but there are two claimants within the Nottinghamshire area. The most obvious is the present Hatfield Chase – an area of carrs (i.e. drained fenland) at the western edge of the Isle of Axholme. The other is near Warsop, for a chantry chapel dedicated to St Edwin is known to have existed between that town and Edwinstowe.

When on 5 August 641 Penda fought another Northumbrian king, Oswald, who was killed in the battle, the latter's body was hacked to pieces. All but his head (which eventually ended its wanderings in St Cuthbert's tomb in Durham cathedral) and his hands were transported to Bardney Abbey beside the River Witham in Lincolnshire. Their possible route may well have been via the Trent and Fossdyke, for a string of churches bears dedications to St Oswald, e.g. Dunham-on-Trent, East Stoke and Ragnall.

Mercia was now the most powerful force in England and its ruler, Penda, had an ambivalent attitude to religion, towards the end of his life claiming to have been converted to Christianity, yet still hedging his bets by continuing his pagan practices until his death in 655. His son and successor Paeda had married the daughter of King Oswui of Northumbria. After the Synod of Whitby in 663 Nottinghamshire was included within the new diocese of Lichfield, which covered the kingdom of Mercia, whose bishop was St Chad (Ceadda).

Although we have some notion from place-name evidence of how many Anglian settlements there were in the county by the seventh century, what we do not know is how many other names were subsequently changed by Danish settlers. Those bearing final elements such as -ing, -ingham and -ington are believed to be amongst the first settlements. Later Anglo-Saxon endings include -ton and -worth. Often the first elements consisted of a personal name. Over forty per cent of all Nottinghamshire place-names come into these two categories. Another 25 per cent bear topographical final elements such as -beck, -field, -focrd, -ley and -well.

Another method of estimating the extent of the early Anglian settlement of the region is by the location of burial sites. However, caution must be exercised here for our present knowledge is very incomplete.

Anglo-Saxon urn from Newark

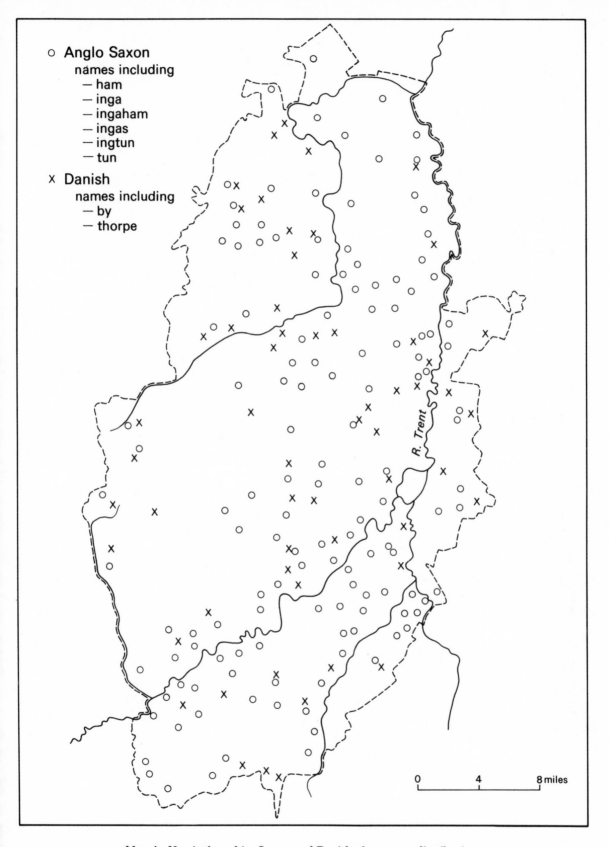

Map 4. Nottinghamshire Saxon and Danish place-name distribution.

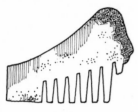

Anglo-Saxon bone comb from Newark

Stapleford cross

Cremation cemeteries containing urns of ashes are known at Holme Pierrepont, Kingston-on-Soar, Netherfield, Newark and Sutton Bonington, whilst interments have been recorded at Aslockton, Bingham, Oxton and Cotgrave. At the last named place an Anglian cemetery was discovered in 1983 on Windmill Hill, where M. W. Bishop excavated 76 burials (including 12 of children). Most of these were roughly orientated in an east-west direction. Nine of the females were accompanied by bronze brooch and/or bead necklaces. Three circular ditches were found, two of which enclosed a central burial of a man with a spear and shield estimated to have been in his mid-twenties.

At Oxton some years ago, excavations revealed that a man of some importance had been laid to rest under a tumulus. Although all the above mentioned sites are situated in the southern half of the county there must surely be some burial sites from this period in the northern half awaiting discovery?

Place-name study can also give us a tentative glimpse of the landscape of Mercian Nottinghamshire. Islands in what was fenland or marshland appear at Bunny (meaning 'reed island'), Cuckney ('Cucca's island'), Holme, Holme Pierrepont and Mattersey. The name Morton also implies fenland. There must have been areas of rushes at Beeston and Tuxford, of heather at Headon, of broom at Bramcote, and of fern at Farndon and Farnsfield. Although documentary evidence of tree species is often post-Conquest, we do have earlier examples such as Eakring (oaks), Bircotes (birch), Ollerton (alders), Linby (limes) and Willoughby (willows).

Likewise the gamut of domesticated animals is reflected at Bulcote and Bulwell (bulls), Calverton (calves), Everton (boars), Gotham (goats), Rampton (rams) and Lambley (lambs). Wheat is the derivation of the names Wheatley and Whatton.

The first mention of Nottingham itself (as Snotengaham) is in the Anglo-Saxon Chronicle of 867. In that year marauding Danes wintered there. They were apparently too powerful a force for the relieving army of King Athelred I of Wessex, who came at the behest of his brother-in-law, King Burgred of Mercia. It is perhaps to this period that the earliest parts of the tower of the church of St John the Evangelist at Carlton-in-Lindrick date. Not every settlement in Mercian times possessed a church, and in many places worship may have taken place around a primitive preaching cross such as those that have survived at Bilsthorpe, Coates (North Leverton), East Bridgford, Hawksworth, Kneesall, Rolleston, Screveton and Shelford. At Stapleford there still stands a very unusual shaft dating from this period on which are apparently carved the symbols of St Luke (an ox) and St John (an eagle).

28

There is evidence of Danish and Viking attacks in the Newark area, where one of their swords has been discovered at Farndon. The first defence works thrown up around Newark may date from those troubled times. But as a result of the signing of the Treaty of Wedmore in 878 by King Alfred of Wessex and the Danish leader, Guthrum, Nottinghamshire became part of the Danelaw, and 'Snotengaham' with Derby, Leicester, Lincoln and Stamford became known as the Five Burghs. These formed a loose federation. Whereas Anglo-Saxon England was divided into hundreds, Danelaw was subdivided into wapentakes. Each of these local government divisions chose its moot place where regular assemblies were held to administer its own area. Nottinghamshire was divided at first into eight such wapentakes, but eventually Lythe (Lide) wapentake was merged with that of Thurgarton, whilst Oswaldbeck became the North Clay division of that of Bassetlaw. We know where some of the moots met. That of Broxtow was on the site of the future Broxtowe Hall in the parish of Bilborough. Thurgarton moot was held at a place called 'Iverishaghe' within Oxton parish. That of Bingham was summoned to assemble at Moot House Pit, a shallow depression beside Fosse Way in the parish of Cropwell Butler. Rushcliffe's is thought to have mustered near Court Hill, Gotham, close by an ancient trackway that linked Thrumpton with Willoughby-on-the-Wolds.

On place-name evidence Danish settlements seem to have been un-evenly distributed in the county. Although there are few ending in -by compared with neighbouring Leicestershire and Lincolnshire, they are mainly in the north-west within Bassetlaw and Broxtow wapentakes. On the other hand there are far more -thorpes, which often imply an outlying settlement or hamlet. Such final elements appear distributed throughout the county, but are especially prevalent in Bassetlaw and Thurgarton wapentakes. In contrast, Bingham and Broxtow have only two and one -thorpe respectively. Other Danish endings include -thwaite and -beck, and the field name 'wong', meaning a wet meadow. In addition there is the Scandinavian influence in place-names containing the present letters k, sc and sk (e.g. Kelham, Eakring, Scofton and Ranskill). The termination -gate from the old word 'geata' meaning a way or street is also evidence of north-west European influence on place-names.

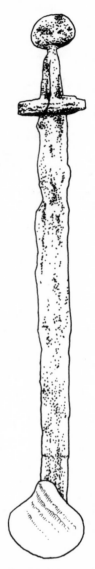

Danish/Viking sword from Farndon

The free Danes were known as 'sokemen' and each probably held between twenty and three hundred acres of arable land. In the words of A. C. Wood they were 'largely independent of the later manorial system'. At the time of the Domesday Survey two centuries later there were approximately 1,500 sokemen within Nottinghamshire. With their families they may have accounted for some thirty per cent of the recorded population of the county in 1086.

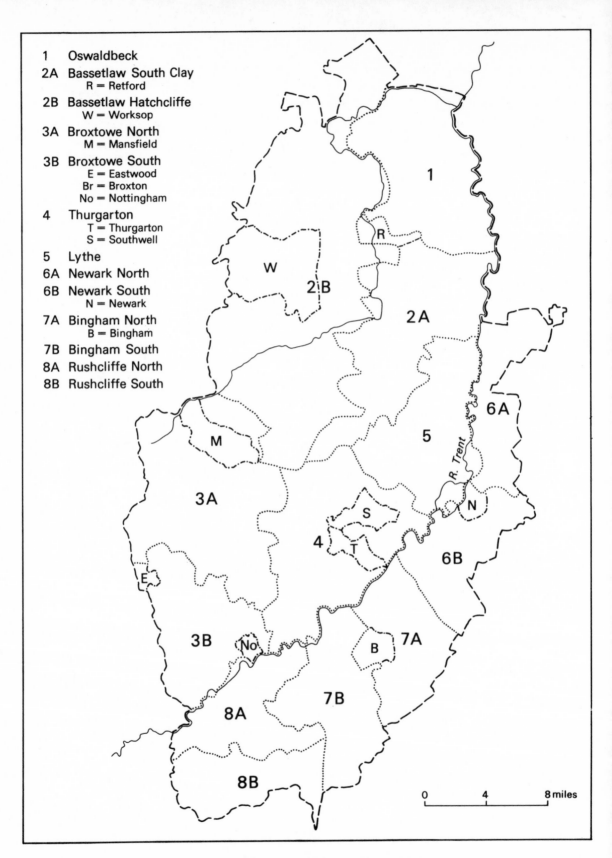

1 Oswaldbeck
2A Bassetlaw South Clay
 R = Retford
2B Bassetlaw Hatchcliffe
 W = Worksop
3A Broxtowe North
 M = Mansfield
3B Broxtowe South
 E = Eastwood
 Br = Broxton
 No = Nottingham
4 Thurgarton
 T = Thurgarton
 S = Southwell
5 Lythe
6A Newark North
6B Newark South
 N = Newark
7A Bingham North
 B = Bingham
7B Bingham South
8A Rushcliffe North
8B Rushcliffe South

Map 5. Danish Wapentakes of Nottinghamshire.

In 910 King Edward the Elder (son of Alfred) began a long campaign to conquer the Danelaw, eventually storming Derby in 917. The following year he besieged Nottingham, which surrendered to him. Before he withdrew from that town he had its defences repaired and left a combined Anglo-Danish garrison in occupation. The Wessex king returned in 920, when he ordered the construction of a bridge across the Trent near the town, with earthworks to guard its approaches at either end.

In 934 his successor Athelstan assembled an army at Nottingham to drive off the Scots. However, four years later the town was back in enemy hands. This time a joint Danish-Norse army forced King Edmund I (the younger brother of Athelstan) to give up all the territory north of Watling Street, thus restoring the Danelaw to its 878 boundaries. But this was a short-lived situation, since in 942 Edmund drove them back as far as the Humber. Certainly Edmund's sons Edwy and Edgar must have had control of Nottinghamshire for they granted extensive estates, mainly in the Southwell area, to two successive Archbishops of York – Osketel and Oswald. It was here that a minster was built along with a residence for the archbishops. Indeed the entire county seems to have been transferred to the diocese of York in 950.

The actual shire of Nottingham was probably created at some point in time between 877 and its first mention in the Anglo-Saxon Chronicle in 1016. However it was certainly part of the extensive lands held by Eadric Streona (his nickname meant 'the greedy one'!) from 1007. He was murdered in 1017 and his body thrown over the city wall of London – possibly on the orders of King Cnut, who had found him to be very untrustworthy. Eadric had joined his sovereign in an invasion of the East Midlands the previous year, and this campaign had resulted in the partitioning of England between Cnut and the young King Edmund II 'Ironside' (son of Athelred II, the 'Unready'). Within a very short period Edmund himself was dead, possibly assassinated by Eadric.

Eadric was succeeded as earldorman of Mercia by his son Leofwine. In his turn Leofwine was succeeded by his far more famous son Leofric, whose wife was the legendary Lady Godiva (or Godgifu), who owned the 'new work' (as distinct from the 'old works' of Crococolana, Ad Pontem and Margidunum – see chapter III). This 'new work' became Newark and guarded the crossings of the Rivers Devon and Trent, as well as the Fosse Way itself. In 1055 Godiva presented Newark to the important monastery of St Mary Stow in Lincolnshire. Already Newark was the second most important town in the shire after Nottingham. The *Dictionary of National Biography* describes Leofric as 'temperate in council, patriotic and religious'.

After Leofric's death in 1057, his son Alfgar briefly held the earldom

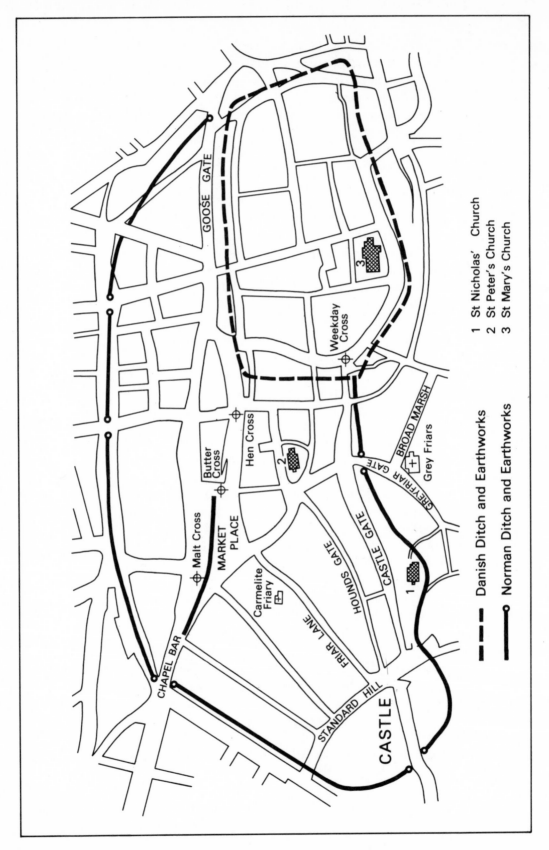

Map 6. Medieval Nottingham.

Danish Ditch and Earthworks
Norman Ditch and Earthworks

1 St Nicholas' Church
2 St Peter's Church
3 St Mary's Church

GOOSE GATE

Weekday Cross

Hen Cross

Butter Cross

Malt Cross

MARKET PLACE

Carmelite Friary

FRIAR LANE

HOUNDS GATE

CASTLE GATE

STANDARD HILL

CHAPEL BAR

CASTLE

GREYFRIAR GATE

BROAD MARSH

Grey Friars

of Mercia, dying in 1062. His eldest son, Eadwine, became the new Earl of Mercia, whilst his brother Morcar was Earl of Northumbria – positions they held at the time of the Norman Conquest a few year later.

A mint was established in Nottingham as early as the reign of Athelstan, after it had been declared to be a royal burgh as a reward for its loyalty to that monarch.

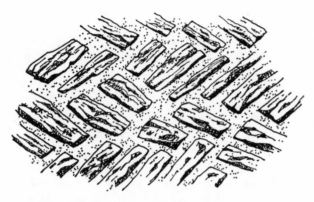

Saxo-Norman herringbone work, Littleborough church

V Domesday Nottinghamshire

Sturton-le-Steeple tower

By January 1066, when King Edward the Confessor died, there were already some extensive landowners in the county, as Domesday Book, completed 20 years later, records. Some of these had Saxon names like Alfric, Alfsi, Wulfuer, Wulfgeat, Wulfric and Wulfsi, whilst others such as Grim, Odincar, Swein, Thorkell, Ulfkell and Ulfketel were probably of Danish extraction. What we cannot always know is whether, for example, the Fran who held land at Keyworth was the same Fran who could be found with estates miles away at East Markham. On the other hand Stori's estates at Gotham, Keyworth, Normanton-on-Soar, Stanton-on-the-Wolds and Sutton Bonington are relatively close together and all may well have been held by the same person. In certain cases a prefix is added to the personal name to differentiate between them. Hence *Young* Swein had land at Bulcote, whereas another Swein had apparently much more land stretching from Radcliff-on-Trent in the south of the county up to Finningley on the borders of Yorkshire. Likewise Wulfsi had estates at Clipstone, Cuckney, Hockerton and Hodstock, whilst *Young* Wulfsi held land at Gonalston, Stapleford and Wollaton. Amongst the estates accredited to Godwin, that at Adbolton refers to him as Godwin *the Priest*, perhaps quite a different person.

In many cases parishes seemed to have been shared, so that Alfwy and Wulfmer had 12 bovates that were taxable at Tuxford, whilst one-and-a-half bovates at Fenton were shared between Grim, Leofric and Wulfheah. Because Nottinghamshire had been part of Danelaw, land measurements are always expressed in the Danish units of carucates, divided into eight bovates, rather than in the more usual Anglo-Saxon terms of hides being divided into virgates. In any case it must always be borne in mind that such measurements as laid down in Domesday are purely notional for assessment purposes and may not correspond with the actual areas under cultivation or other land use.

On the eve of the Norman invasion there were already some land-owners with Norman names, e.g. Reginald (Clarborough, Hawton and Kirton), Richard (Keyworth and Kingston-on-Soar) and William (Widmerspool).

Saxo-Norman door-way, Markham Clinton

As with other counties that came within Danelaw there were considerable numbers of free peasants called sokemen in the mid-11th century. Throughout Nottinghamshire as a whole they made up 32.1 per cent of all tenants listed in Domesday, but in the western wapentakes of Broxtow and Thurgarton they accounted for only 13.5 per cent and 17.3 per cent respectively, whereas in the north-eastern wapentake of Oswaldbeck they formed a slight majority of all tenants at 51.8 per cent. King Edward himself had held land in every wapentake apart from Thurgarton. On these royal estates the sokemen made up 31.5 per cent of the tenants.

Carved doorway, Hawton church

The largest group mentioned in Domesday were the villeins, who were tied to their land in return for labour services to the local lord of the manor. This class represented 45.3 per cent countywide, increasing to 48.8 per cent on the royal manors. But here again there were considerable variations between wapentakes. For instance, whereas they formed the largest group by far in Broxtow (62.9 per cent) and Thurgarton (57.3 per cent) their lowest percentage was to be found in Oswaldbeck at 22.9 per cent. The third and by far the smallest group were the bordars (the equivalent of the cottars in the Anglo-Saxon shires) They were the smallholders, who eked out a living by providing the craft element in their local communities as carpenters, blacksmiths, wheelwrights, etc.

Domesday mentions churches although, unlike some other counties, no dedications are referred to. In a few instances two churches are listed for the same village; this was sometimes because such a community was divided into two separate manors under the feudal system. So both Hawton and Sutton-in-Ashfield had two places of worship. On the other hand some places had only half a church (e.g. Cotgrave, Kneeton, Langar and Leverton), whilst Bole had only one-quarter of a church! This was probably because, as there was no actual church established locally, tithes and other ecclesiastical fees had to be paid to a central church in that proportion. However, we do know on architectural evidence that not all existing places of worship were listed in Domesday. Thus there are features pre-dating 1086 to be found in the churches at Askham, Carburton, Hawksworth and Littleborough, for example. Similarly, although no church is mentioned for Linby, a priest is listed for this place, and the present parish church of St Michael does have a simple (i.e. early) Norman south doorway.

As there were no windmills in England before the reign of Henry II (1154-1189) the only methods of grinding grain into flour were by handmills and watermills. So it is the latter which are mentioned in Domesday. In several instances two such mills are listed for one settlement, but again it must be remembered that this may be due to a parish being divided into more than one manor, or it may be because most

Priest on a Saxo-Norman font, Markham Clinton

watermills would have been rather small and primitive structures, perhaps unable to cope with all the demands made on them. Thus there were two mills at West Drayton, whilst Epperstone and Woodborough shared four. At Kingston-on-Soar and Stanford-on-Soar only the sites of mills are mentioned (had they been burnt down?), whilst at Clipstone there is the strange entry for *half* a mill site.

Fisheries came into two categories. The first was obviously those connected with rivers, and in particular the Trent, as at Laneham, Newark, Norwell and South Muskham. In 1973 a medieval fish weir was investigated at Colwick. This was made of six rows of oak and holly posts forming a 'V', the neck of which pointed downstream. This was constructed more than likely to ensnare eels during their autumnal migration in the river. Carbon 14 dating suggests that this weir was built in the Trent in the 12th century. In construction it was similar to others known from Clifton, Dunham-on-Trent, Holme Pierrepont and Netherfield. At Saundby, Domesday Book specifically refers to the King's fishery at Bycar's Dyke. Eels were certainly regarded as a delicacy at this period and 200 of them are listed at West Burton. Away from the Trent at Gringley-on-the-Hill as many as 1,000 eels are mentioned. These may well have been bred in artificial ponds.

In some counties such as Yorkshire the term 'waste' in Domesday is a sure indication that that particular settlement had been laid waste by William I following the Northern Rebellion of 1067. However, in Nottinghamshire, the term refers to land unsuitable for arable farming. In Sherwood Forest and its environs this is especially true (e.g. Babworth, Normanton-by-Clumber, Perlethorpe and Ranby). Indeed proof of this comes at Headon, a place-name meaning 'heather', where 'waste' is recorded.

As a result of the Norman Conquest few of the land-holders of January 1066 were left in occupation. A. C. Wood has suggested that some may have perished fighting for Harold II against his half-brother Testig and King Harold Hardrada at the battle of Gate Fulford (near York) on 20 September 1066, three weeks before the crucial battle of Hastings. As well as King William himself, by 1086 the Archbishop of York held extensive estates in the county, whilst Newark wapentake was dominated by the newly-appointed Bishop Remigius of Lincoln, who held lands previously in the hands of his predecessors, the bishops of Dorchester-on-Thames. Again St Peter's Abbey, Peterborough, still possessed estates at Collingham and North Muskham. Several of the new Norman tenants-in-chief had been given extensive grants of land in neighbouring Lincolnshire, e.g. Count Alan, Earl Hugh and Gilbert of Ghent. Others made Nottinghamshire their power base, of whom one of the most

Norman arcading, Southwell Minster

powerful was William Peverel, who was rewarded with land in no less than 49 manors stretching from Barton-in-Fabis in the south of the county to Sibthorpe in the north-east. In particular he was given by King William the important feudal fief known as the Honour of Nottingham and was ordered by his sovereign to erect a castle on the rock there so that, in William Camden's later words, he could 'bridle the English'.

14th-century 'pepperbox' dovecote, Sibthorpe

After the murder of Earl Edwin of Mercia in 1071 the Conqueror placed the house of Ferrers (now Earls of Derby) in overall charge of Nottinghamshire, which gave them the unofficial right to call themselves Earls of Nottinghamshire as well. But in fact the first Earl, Henry, only had three holdings in this county in 1086, viz. Leake, Sutton Bonington and Willoughby-on-the-Wolds.

Roger de Busli held land in no less than 107 manors, distributed throughout every wapentake except that of Lythe. However, there was a particular concentration of his estates within Bassetlaw, which accounted for 42 of them. The widespread nature of de Busli's lands is demonstrated by the fact that within them lay three places called Normanton (-on-Soar, -on-Trent and -on-the-Wolds). His manor of Egmanton lay cheek-by-jowl with that of Geoffrey Alselin at Laxton. Although most of his lands were to be found in Bassetlaw and Lythe wapentakes, he also held manors in those of Bingham and Thurgarton.

Apart from Nottingham, the only other town in the county at the time of the compilation of Domesday was Newark. Here Bishop Remigius had 56 burgesses amongst his tenants, along with 42 villeins, but only four bordars. As well as one mill and a fishery, there appear to be as many as 10 churches. However these and their eight accompanying priests are because this is an episcopal manor.

Bearing in mind that people do not want to give the impression to those in a position to tax them that they are doing well, and that our records are not complete for the estimated value of all the land in the county, we discover that, in the 296 cases where this data was forthcoming, in 58.4 per cent of such cases a loss in value is registered compared with the figure for 1066. Indeed in Lythe wapentake this rises to a massive 83.3 per cent and it is over 70 per cent in Bassetlaw, Broxtow and Newark wapentakes. Only Oswaldbeck at 2.1 per cent claimed to be relatively better off under the militant William than under the holy Edward. On the other hand 24.7 per cent of places reckoned that there had been no change in value, with a mere 16.9 per cent confessing to an improvement. However, unlike Yorkshire, no community was assessed as being worth nothing. There appears to be no perceptible geographical pattern for these returns.

VI Sherwood Forest

Entrance to Clumber Park

The earliest extant Pipe Roll dates from 1130 and mentions Sherwood. This place-name implies a common wood belonging to the whole shire. It is not until the reign of Edward I (1272-1307) that specific documents dealing exclusively with Sherwood appear, although its existence as a royal hunting ground is likely to date back to soon after the Norman Conquest. Unlike certain other medieval royal forests, Sherwood was not used as such by Edward the Confessor (1042-1066). Yet there is evidence in Domesday Book that it existed at that time.

In 1086 it covered approximately twenty per cent of Nottinghamshire, being 20 miles long by eight miles wide – a vast area of some 160 square miles of what is described as 'waste' and 'woodland pasture'. Both were necessary, for animals like deer and wild boar needed the latter as cover, whilst hunters required the former for the kill, once they had driven the beasts from amongst the oak and beech woods. The measurements of the waste are not given, but those of the woodland pastures are expressed in leagues (i.e. one-and-a-half miles) and furlongs (220 yards). Hence at Bothamsall there was both waste and woodland that was half a league in length by four furlongs in width (i.e. covering 240 acres). Edwinstowe's woodland was half a league square (i.e. 360 acres), whereas Clumber had waste and woodland which was a mere two furlongs by one furlong in extent (i.e. 20 acres). Adjacent Normanton had slightly more with an area that measured three furlongs by two furlongs (i.e. 30 acres) in addition to waste. Perhaps the entry for Clipstone emphasises best the nature of the forest as it recorded that there was 'woodland pastures *in places* 1 league long and 1 wide' (author's italics): a considerable 1,440 acres, albeit only the average size of parishes in that part of the county.

The fact that the value of Clumber in 1086 was assessed at only one-fifth of its pre-Conquest estimate may indicate that Sherwood had not become a royal hunting forest by that date. However, by the reign of Henry II (1154-1189) there was a hunting lodge at Clipstone, although known to future generations as King John's Palace. Sir Nikolaus Pevsner placed its surviving masonry as possibly 12th century.

There was a castle at Cuckney on the edge of the Forest, probably one of the so-called 'adulterine' (or illegal) structures of the reign of Stephen (1135-1154) and attributed to Thomas of Cuckney. At Bothamsall there was a wooden Norman castle overlooking the Meden valley on the other side of the Forest; its earthworks remain. It was situated on that portion of Sherwood which fell within the confines of the vast estates of Roger de Busli: a reminder that not all the Forest was owned by the crown, although all of it came within the jurisdiction of the Forest Laws.

These laws were administered by the royal Justiciar for the Forests Yon Side Trent, and covered not only the protection of game, but also the carrying of weapons in the area by anybody except bona fide travellers, who were themselves restricted to using the highways that traversed the woodlands and waste. These statutes covered in addition such matters as oaks growing in the Forest, assarts created by clearing parts of Sherwood for cultivation as the population slowly increased, buildings erected there and the use of both woodlands and waste for grazing cattle and swine.

Foresters and woodwards had the right to arrest any trespassers. Such offenders were either forced to give pledges to appear at the next attachment or were kept in custody until they could be presented before a verderers' court. These were held every six weeks in various locations within Sherwood. The court would meet at Linby on a Monday, Calverton on a Wednesday, Mansfield on a Thursday and Edwinstowe on a Friday.

However, in 1217 as one of the results of Magna Carta and the ensuing civil war, such barbarities as blinding those found guilty of breaking the Forest Laws or the maiming of criminals by the amputation of fingers or the complete hand were replaced by more humane punishments such as fines and imprisonment. Between 1287 and 1334 no Forest Eyres (the courts which dealt with major breaches of the Forest Laws) were held. In any case, as G. D. Turner has pointed out, such courts had become 'almost as much a financial assembly as a court of law'. And it was their financial attraction that prevented successive sovereigns from allowing deforestation to take place.

No chapter on Sherwood would be complete without some consideration of the story of Robin Hood. Professor J. C. Holt (1982) has examined many of the claimants of this elusive name. He has come to the conclusion that the famous outlaw 'cannot be identified. There is a quiverful of possible Robin Hoods. Even the likeliest is little better than a shot in the gloaming.' There are mentions of one Robin Hood in the Pipe Rolls of 1225/6, 1228, 1230 and 1231. However, he is called Robert Hod and appears to be a fugitive from the justice administered by the

Robin Hood

39

Little John

Sheriff of *Yorkshire*. Indeed in the 'Lytell Geste of Robyn Hode' the action takes place in the Wakefield area, instead of in Sherwood. This tale is written in the language of the 14th century, although the earliest extant copies of it date from the following century. Nevertheless in this particular version Robin does indeed slay the Sheriff of Nottingham, albeit in the reign of a certain King Edward. Now the only king of that name to pass through the area was Edward II in 1323. In this story Robin is accompanied by his faithful companions Little John, Will Scarlock and Much (the miller's son). Such popular characters as Friar Tuck and Maid Marian seem to have been added to the tales at a much later date. Friar Tuck may have been the alias of one Robert Stafford of Lindfield (near Haywards Heath, Sussex) who gathered around him a band of malefactors in the early 15th century. Near Lindfield is the village of Fletching, where the compounded surname of Robynhood is recorded several times after 1296. Maid Marian appears to have been a romantic addition in Tudor times. In the long pastoral poem 'Piers the Ploughman' (written *c*.1377) occurs the line

'Ich can rymes of Robin Hood'

Whoever Robin Hood was, he was certainly neither a dispossessed knight nor the Earl of Huntingdon in disguise. He is much more likely to have been a member of the yeoman classes.

The felling of oaks for use in building was strictly controlled and royal permission was necessary, as in the case of the Grey Friars of Nottingham in the early 13th century for the erection of their chapel. A similar grant was made at a later date to the White Friars of that city. Trees were also allowed to be cut down in certain cases for the reconstruction of churches and for the siege engines.

It is believed that up until the end of the 15th century the area of Sherwood Forest was approximately 100,000 acres. However, a survey carried out in 1609 showed that by then its extent had been reduced to 89,405 acres. Of this total, 44,839 acres had already been enclosed, leaving 35,080 acres unenclosed, together with 9,486 acres of woodlands. There were four significant parks within the Forest; Clipston (1,583 acres), Bestwood (3,672 acres), Bulwell (326 acres) and Nottingham (129 acres). A count of oaks was also taken in 1609 and the aggregate, the epitomy of Sherwood, was 49,909 trees. Another count seven years later revealed that there were 1,263 red deer roaming in the Forest. Changes were on the way; in August 1624, a serious fire destroyed an area in excess of 4,000 acres. Then, during the Commonwealth period (1649-60), the Navy was increased in size to combat the Dutch, and many oaks were felled for ship construction. At that time, as the monarchy had been abolished, Sherwood was no longer regarded as a royal hunting estate and consequently many animals were slaughtered. At the Restoration a royal warrant was issued in November 1661 for the import from Germany of replacement stocks of red and fallow deer. Again there was a demand for oak timber, this time for the peaceful purpose of rebuilding St Paul's Cathedral after the Great Fire of 1666. These trees were especially taken from the estates of the Duke of Newcastle, a personal friend of Charles II, at Welbeck Abbey.

Meanwhile the wild parts of the Forest continued to diminish. Three thousand acres became the new Clumber Park created by the Earl of Clare (later to succeed to the dukedom of Newcastle), which was later expanded by a further 1,000 acres. Other enclosures were for agricultural purposes, for example, at Blidworth in the mid-18th century. Acts passed in 1789 and 1796 brought another 8,248 acres into cultivation at Arnold, Kirby-in-Ashfield, Lenton, Radford and Sutton-in-Ashfield. Again, the character of the Forest was changing with the introduction of Scotch firs, which thrived on the sandy soil. Nevertheless by the middle of the last century there was a change in policy, to reafforestation with a mixture of species such as birch, larch, pine, as well as the traditional oaks.

The discovery of the tourist potential of Sherwood started in the 19th century with the advent of the wagonette and horse-drawn charabanc, and has continued into this century with their motorised equivalents, together with widespread private car ownership. The fact that the Forest lies on the doorsteps of the city of Nottingham and the conurbation that has grown up between there and Mansfield has increased its appeal for picknickers, hikers and nature lovers. In recent years Nottinghamshire County Council, recognising this asset, has provided and staffed a Visitors' Centre near Edwinstowe, which includes exhibitions on the history of the Forest.

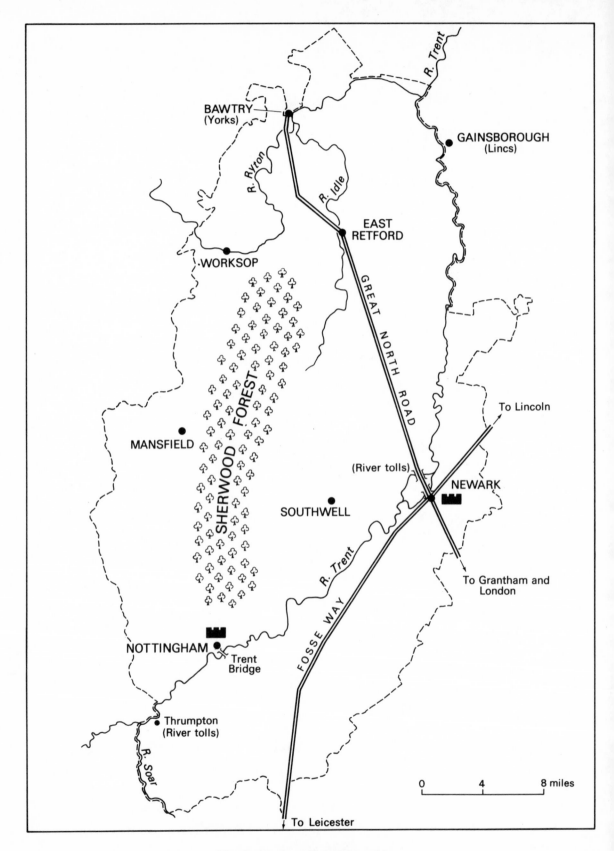

Map 7. Medieval Nottinghamshire.

VII Medieval Towns and Trade

From Domesday we learn that Nottingham had 173 burgesses and 19 villeins living there before the Conquest. Hugh, son of Baldric the Sheriff, had built a further 13 houses on Earl Tosti's land within the new borough. Indeed, as well as William Peverel, whom we have come across in chapter V, and who had charge of the newly erected royal castle, some of the county's other principal tenants-in-chief had a foothold in the town. For example Roger de Busli had 11 houses there in three separate plots, whilst Geoffrey Alselin had 21 houses.

Medieval tub font, West Markham

There is an interesting note to the effect that there were 17 houses, plus six others in the Borough ditch, indicating the growth of a suburb outside the earthworks that marked the town's limits. This was the nucleus of what became known as the 'Norman borough' (alias the 'New' or 'French' town) to be distinguished from the 'Old' or 'English borough'. Such terms were employed until at least the mid-15th century. Each of these boroughs had its own code of laws, and even its own quarter sessions until the close of the 17th century. Yet they shared a common market place, albeit divided by a wall until 1713!

More important is the recording of 48 merchants' houses, demonstrative of Nottingham's growing importance as a trading town along the Trent valley. The tributary River Leam was provided with a wooden quay, built by the Franciscan Friars in the 13th century. The Trent comes in for especial mention in Domesday, viz. 'The river Trent and the dyke [the Leam?] and the road to York are so protected that if anyone hinders the passage of ships or if anyone ploughs or makes a dyke within 2 perches [i.e. 11 yards] of the King's road, he has to pay a fine of £8'. This was a colossal sum in those days, indicative of the vital importance of these highways by land and water to the town.

The only church in Norman times in Nottingham was St Mary's, and this lay within the King's lordship. It was valued at 100 shillings per annum. Altard the priest is listed as holding two houses. Apart from one fragment of two 12th-century arches built into the wall of a warehouse in Broadway, nothing remains of this edifice, since the present St Mary's is almost entirely a 15th-century structure, and is the second largest

Medieval gargoyle

43

church in the county. Within a decade of the compilation of Domesday Book the parish churches of St Peter and of St Nicholas (the latter being a patron saint of seamen, a significant dedication in the light of Nottingham's role as a trading centre) had also been built.

In the summer of 1067 William I (1066-1087) came to the town with his army en route to York to crush the Northern Rebellion. It was on this occasion that he ordered William Peverel to erect a castle to protect the town and to guard the passage along the Trent. However, Peverel and his successors were only royal castellans of this fortress and could not number it amongst their possessions.

During the Civil War between King Stephen (1135-1154) and his cousin Empress Maud (alias Matilda), the daughter of Henry I (1100-1135), Robert, Earl of Gloucester (Maud's half-brother) raided the town in 1140. He failed to storm the castle and, in angry frustration, he sacked Nottingham itself. In the following year, after Stephen's capture at the Battle of Lincoln, Maud forced Peverel (who had been taken prisoner in that same battle) to hand over the castle to William Pegenal of Bingham, who would act as custodian on her behalf. Nevertheless, once he had been released, Peverel surprised the garrison and repossessed this bastion on behalf of the King. When in 1153 Maud's son Henry of Anjou in his turn laid siege to Nottingham, Peverel set fire to the town in a scorched earth policy in order to drive out his opponent. In 1154 the Count of Anjou became King Henry II (1154-1189) and deprived Peverel of his post, replacing him with Ranulf, Earl of Chester. But Peverel's days were not yet ended, for he is suspected of having had Ranulf poisoned, reinstating himself in the castle, before being forced to flee to sanctuary at nearby Lenton Priory disguised as a monk, when his royal master returned to the town in February 1155.

However, Nottingham's trials were not yet over, for in May 1174 William de Ferrers, Earl of Derby, seized and plundered the town. Whilst Richard I (1189-1199) was on the Third Crusade, his younger brother John was given responsibility for six counties, including Nottinghamshire. In 1192 John managed to wrest control of the castle from Richard's Justiciar, Bishop William Longchamp. But on 25 March 1194 Richard returned to the town and demanded its surrender from Ralph Murdoc and William de Wendevay, who held it on behalf of John. Three days later it capitulated to the King. In time this episode became woven into the tales of Robin Hood which were examined in the previous chapter.

During the Barons' Wars the castle was held for Simon de Montfort, but surrendered to the forces of King Henry III (1216-1272), who appointed John de Grey as royal constable there. However, after the

Nottingham Castle barbican

44

King had been captured following the Battle of Lewes on 14 May 1264, de Montfort repossessed the fortress, putting Hugh Le Despenser in charge of it.

During these troubled times the town's walls were started, although work appears to have gone on until 1334 and may not even then have been completed. They may have stood some 30 feet high in places and have been up to seven feet thick.

Perhaps the most famous incident in the castle's medieval history took place on 19 October 1330, when Roger Mortimer, Earl of March and the lover of Queen Mother Isabella and one of the regicides of King Edward II (1307-1327), was surprised and arrested there. One of his captors, William de Eland of Algarthorpe, was rewarded by the young King Edward III (1327-1377) with the appointment of constable of the castle.

As we have seen above, Nottingham's prosperity depended greatly on trade along the Trent, and a confirmatory charter of Henry II gave the town the right to exact tolls on shipping between Thrumpton (upstream and on the shire boundary) and Newark. The maintenance of the Trent Bridge was equally important to the town, and in both 1231 and 1234 Henry III gave permission for stone to be quarried in Nottingham for this purpose. In the following decade four Sherwood oaks were allocated for repair work to this essential structure. Yet in 1311 and again in 1335 there were reports of its dangerous condition. Two Bridgemasters were appointed from 1374, but keeping this vital link in good shape relied heavily on charitable donations by those who prayed at the little chapel of St James (the patron saint of pilgrims) on the bridge itself, and also on legacies.

Henry II's charter also covered the granting of Friday and Saturday markets to the town, along with a local monopoly in the manufacture of dyed cloth. In 1284 Edward I (1272-1307) gave Nottingham the additional right to elect a mayor 'to be set over the bailiffs and others of the said borough in everything pertaining to the government and advantage of the said town'. At the same time there was a grant for the holding of a fair for 15 days annually around the Feast of St Edmund (20 November).

The commerce of the town was aided by the Jewish community, who dwelt in a ghetto between the Castle Gate and Hounds Gate, and had their own synagogue in Lister Gate. Although free from the persecutions which took place elsewhere such as in Lincoln, an assessment in 1255 showed them as fewer in number than in 17 other English towns and cities with similar communities. But after 1264 anti-semitism spread to Nottingham, and finally in 1290 the Jews were expelled nationwide by

Edward I. Already their places as money-lenders were being taken by Italians. Thus in Henry III's reign David the Lombard and Amyot le Limberd were in business in the town. It was not only Nottingham merchants who borrowed money from the local Jews. Newark (which did not have a Jewish ghetto) had businessmen who sought loans from Eleasar and Hasna of Nottingham in 1193.

Nottingham sent two burgesses to represent the town at Edward I's so-called 'Model Parliament' of 1295. Parliament itself was held in Nottingham in 1336 and perhaps six years earlier, as the name Parliament Street reminds us today.

The second most important town in the county in the Middle Ages was Newark. This had been replanned by Bishop Alexander the Magnificent of Lincoln, who was a great builder in the reign of Henry I. He built one of his castles on the banks of the River Devon, where it guarded the crossing of that river by the diverted Fosseway. Alexander's successor, Bishop Robert Chesney, had the right to mint coins in the town. Earl Roger of Salisbury, who was Bishop Alexander's father, joined with his son in quarrelling with King Stephen, and this led to the loss of the castle to royal forces in 1139.

Later, in October 1216, Newark Castle became the deathbed of King John, after he had arrived there from Swineshead in Lincolnshire, where according to the contemporary chronicler John Hardyng,

> 'Some bookes sayen he poisoned was to dead
> Of plummes so sittyng at his meat',

Medieval stone king, Newark church

an incident that Shakespeare incorporated into his play *King John*. As soon as he reached Newark John made his will, passing away on 19 October. His body was conveyed to Worcester Cathedral for burial, according to arrangements made some time previously with the Bishop of that diocese.

During the Civil War that started when Pope Innocent III had declared against John and in favour of the Dauphin Louis of France (the future Louis VIII), Newark Castle was besieged by William Marshall with 400 knights and 250 crossbowmen, and he ousted one of King John's mercenaries. In the 13th century the castle became a popular stopping place for King Edward I as he travelled between England and Scotland. In the castle today there is nothing of Bishop Alexander's original structure, although there are remnants of the work ordered by Bishop Geoffrey Plantagenet, the illegitimate son of Henry II, along with some of the buildings erected in the 13th century. The square-headed windows that face the river, however, date from its last restoration under the auspices of an Earl of Rutland in 1587.

Newark had early defence works and walls were added to these at a

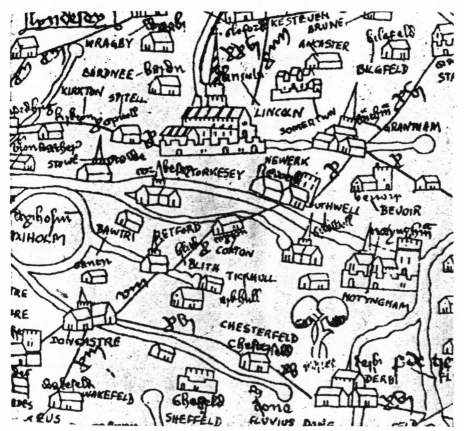

Nottinghamshire in the 14th century, from an early map in the Bodleian Library

later date. However, it was not primarily a fortress town, but an important commercial centre, even though it was denied the right to have its own burgesses sitting in the Commons until the reign of Charles II (1660-1685), a reward for their loyalty to his father, who made Newark one of his principal bases during the Civil War (see chapter XII). Perhaps it was felt that Newark was sufficiently represented through its landlord the Bishop of Lincoln sitting in the upper house? Or maybe the borough did not possess powerful enough friends amongst the nobility?

St Mary Magdalen church dominates the Newark skyline today as it has done certainly since it was rebuilt in the 15th century, when it became the largest parish church in Nottinghamshire. Its main east-west axis is 222 feet (68 m), whilst its steeple rises to a height of 252 feet (77 m), only exceeded in the East Midlands by St Wulfram's in nearby

Grantham (272 feet) and St James's at Louth (295 feet). By the 14th century the town's growing wealth was demonstrated when the chantries were added to the church's interior (e.g. Durant's in 1326, Maud Sawce-mere's in 1330, Robert de Bosco's in 1331). St Mary Magdalen's also possesses one of the largest monumental brasses in England, that of Alan Fleming, a foreign merchant, who died here in 1363. Something of what must have been the late-medieval splendour of the very large Market Place can still be seen in the beautifully-restored *White Hart Inn*, dating back to the 14th century, its timber-framed upright posts being covered with small plaster figures of saints and angels.

According to Domesday Book, Mansfield had been largely owned by King Edward the Confessor, and had therefore passed into the hands of the Conqueror. This was not very auspicious for its future as an important borough expecting to be reasonably free to manage its own affairs. It had few freemen in 1086 too – only five sokemen, compared with 35 villeins and 20 bordars. However, it did possess a mill, a fishery and two churches (each with a priest). Of these latter structures, only the Norman steeple of St Peter's has survived, the remainder having been rebuilt *c*.1300.

East Retford grew from even less promising beginnings, for in 1086 it was part of the lands held by Roger de Busli. The River Idle, neverthe-less, provided a vital link to the outside world, and its market attracted the people who dwelt in Sherwood as well as those who resided in the fenny carrs to the north of the town. M. W. Bishop believes that East Retford was carved out of Clarborough parish *c*.1105 as a new town with the blessing of Henry I. It was on a 120-acre site at the junction of the parishes of Clarborough, Ordsall and West Retford: the classic example of such a market being established (as at Brigg in Lincolnshire, for example). It took a further step forward in 1225 when the burgesses of Nottingham leased their tolls to the burgesses of this much smaller town. A generation later, in 1259, a royal charter granted East Retford a fair for the octave of the Feast of the Holy Trinity. In other words the fair could last for four days on either side of Trinity Sunday. In 1313 this fair was moved to the Feast of St Gregory (3 September), a much more convenient date for planning since, unlike Holy Trinity Day, it was not a moveable feast. Later still an additional six-day fair was instituted for the octave of St Margaret's Day (16 November). Another charter issued in 1276 allowed the burgesses to elect two bailiffs them-selves instead of having to accept royal appointees. Although the town was represented in the Parliament of 1315, poverty was pleaded to exempt the burgesses from sending M.P.s in future, and the borough did not regain its seats until 1571.

Seal of East Retford borough

9. (*above*) *Ye Old Trip To Jerusalem* built against the Castle Rock in Nottingham claims to be one of the oldest inns in England.

10. (*right*) Seen boarded up in 1987, *Ye Flying Horse* Inn, Poultry, next to Nottingham's Council House, was first opened in 1483.

11. (*above*) The Major Oak, Sherwood Forest, is believed to be 650 years old and is likely to be covered by a plastic dome shortly to preserve it.

12. (*left*) Robin Hood's statue in the ditch of Nottingham Castle.

13. (*above*) The ruins of King John's so-called
'Palace' (in fact a hunting lodge) at Clipstone in
Sherwood Forest. Engraved by Sparrow in 1784.

14. (*right*) Nottingham Castle: having been built
in its present form by the Duke of Newcastle two
centuries earlier, it was restored in 1878.

15. The church of St Mary Magdalen dominates the large Newark market place. It has an Early English spire 252 feet high.

16. The perpendicular nave and chancel of St Mary Magdalen's church, Newark.

17. Newark Castle on the banks of the River Devon has been a ruin since its days as a royalist stronghold in the Civil War.

The large Early English-style church of St Swithin was mainly rebuilt during its restoration in 1855 but, with its central medieval tower (which collapsed in 1651), it must have been an imposing sight as well as being an outward manifestation of the town's success – in spite of pleas to the contrary!

Gargoyle, Hawksworth

Worksop was also one of Roger de Busli's possessions, until these were escheated to the crown in the reign of William II (1087-1100), after he had died without heirs. According to Domesday, Worksop contained 22 sokemen, 24 villeins and eight bordars, but it did not begin to grow until the foundation of a Cluniac priory there on 3 March 1103 (see chapter IX).

Wool, Cloth and Hose

It was said that the 'Princely Trent' was the cause of a thriving wool industry being based in medieval Newark and Nottingham, especially during the 14th century. In 1299 Thomas de Cuckney turned a 60-acre field into a sheep walk for no less than 700 animals. However as late as 1517/18 an Enquiry into Enclosures found that only 4,470 acres of the county had been so treated – less than one per cent of the total area of Nottinghamshire. Some such conversions as at Car Colston, Sibthorpe and Screveton did not take place until the reign of Elizabeth I.

John Barton of Holme was a Newark wool merchant, and when he died the following verse was inscribed on his memorial window:

'I thank God and ever shall
It is the sheepe hath payed for all'.

Although there were flourishing local families like the Durants, the Keysers and the Stuffyns engaged in this trade, there were also other wool merchants who were based elsewhere in England, e.g. Hardulf de Barton of Kingston-upon-Hull and Thomas Tyrwhitt of Beverley. In addition there were foreign merchants like Godekin de Revel (Tallinn, Estonia) and the German Hildegrand Sudermann. The town's wool trade was controlled by the mayor and 24 aldermen.

At the commencement of his reign King John issued a charter to Nottingham which amongst other things granted permission for the merchants to establish their own gild in the town, and to be exempt from paying tolls throughout the whole of the king's territories.

One of the complaints of the Newark merchants in 1369 was that they were being forced to export their wool through the faraway port of Boston instead of the much nearer one of Lincoln. Nevertheless many of these merchants were sufficiently rich to be able to lend money to the crown. Amongst them were John le Colier and Matilda Sausmer. Robert de Beghton and Roger de Bothole of Nottingham were also royal creditors.

As the Middle Ages progressed not only did the English wool trade expand, but so did the native cloth industry. Nottinghamshire cloth was referred to as 'northern cloth', since it was manufactured yon side of Trent. A 'piece' of this cloth was supposed to measure between 23 and 25 yards in length and to weigh around 46 lbs. A 'half piece' or 'dozen' was half that length at 12 or 13 yards and weighed 37 lbs.

Lenton Fair (established in 1300) was the greatest cloth market in the county, and in 1355 Nottingham itself was created a *cloth* staple town, though not a wool staple.

The Nottingham Gild of Weavers dated back to the reign of Henry II. As with Nottingham's dyers, no outsider could practise the craft within 10 leagues (15 miles) of the town. Presumably the dyers were located along Lister Gate – the word 'lister' meaning a 'dyer'. The dyers of Newark paid a tax to Henry II for their monopoly. One particularly popular type of medieval cloth was known as the kersey (named after a village in Suffolk near Lavenham). In 1496 these were available dyed in green, black or watchet (blue), although white kerseys were also available.

Born at Calverton in the middle of the 16th century, William Lee was educated at Christ's College, Cambridge, and subsequently entered the Anglican priesthood. Eventually he became the incumbent of his home village. He was a very inventive man and spent much of his time trying to perfect a machine which would knit silk stockings. In 1589 he moved with his invention to Bunhill Fields in London. Nine years later he presented to Elizabeth I a pair of silk stockings which he had knitted on his improved apparatus. However, neither she nor her successor James I thought fit to encourage Lee since they feared trouble from redundant hand knitters. So Lee emigrated to France and set up his machinery in Rouen, where he interested King Henri IV in his products. He died in 1610 soon after the assassination of that French monarch. His brother James then returned to Nottinghamshire and entered into a partnership with one Aston, a miller of Thoroton.

By 1641 there were two master hosiers manufacturing maching-knitted stockings in Nottingham. By 1664 there were 200 workmen employed on 100 such frames. Sixty per cent of their products were made of silk. By 1700 the number of these machines had quadrupled.

In 1597, whilst the Lee brothers were experimenting with hosiery, Roger Clarke was weaving band lace in Nottingham, although most of the operatives in this craft were traditionally women.

Bingham market cross

VIII   The Wars of the Roses

When King Henry VI raised Nottingham to county status in 1448, recognising the borough as a 'perpetual incorporated community', nobody could have imagined that within a decade the loyalties of the nobility and knights of the area would be tested to the uttermost by a prolonged (if intermittent) and blood-soaked dynastic conflict. The Wars of the Roses were dynastic in origin and had several causes. In the first instance the fact that King Edward III had six sons who survived into adulthood is significant, since by the mid-14th century there were many of royal blood amongst the aristocracy. Secondly, the country had become destabilised during the long minority of King Henry VI, who succeeded to the throne in 1422 at the tender age of six months. His uncles, who were supposed to have protected him and his realm, fell out amongst themselves. Thirdly, when Henry did assume his royal powers at the end of his minority he became dominated by his ruthless, arrogant and hated queen Margaret of Anjou, whose French birth was an added bone of contention. Finally, the Hundred Years War, which had included some notable English victories at Crecy (1346), Poitiers (1356) and Agincourt (1415), ended in abject humiliation at the hands of the French.

Collingham cross

On the side of King Henry VI fought such local magnates as the Earl of Shrewsbury, Viscount Beaumont, Lord Lovel, Lord Roos of Belvoir, Sir Gervase Clinton and Sir Robert Strelley. Amongst those actively supporting the Yorkists were Lord Cromwell, Lord Scrope, Sir Richard Illingworth (of Bunny), Sir Robert Markham and Sir Henry Pierrepont. Of the above named, both Roos and Clinton were beheaded, whilst Cromwell was killed at the second Battle of Barnet in 1471.

Prior to the Battle of Wakefield in 1460 there was a skirmish between a force led by Richard, Duke of York and the Lancastrian vanguard near Worksop.

Later King Edward IV visited Nottingham on several occasions during the period 1469-71, and ordered the erection of a great octagonal tower at the castle. This work was completed by his brother King Richard III, who created William, Lord Berkeley, Earl of Nottingham in 1483.

Perpendicular church tower, Keyworth

Berkeley's mother had been the co-heiress of the Mowbray family who had held this earldom since 1377. Richard III himself was in Nottingham on 22 June 1485 on his way to stay at his hunting lodge at Bestwood. It was whilst he was there on 11 August that he learned that his arch-enemy Henry Tudor had landed an army at Milford Haven. The King left Nottingham five days later to perish on Bosworth Field on the 22 August. Amongst those who fought on his side on that fateful day was Sir John Byron.

However, it was the plot to place the pretender Lambert Simnel on the throne that most affected the county during the Wars of the Roses. The Lancastrian supporters of this young man announced that he was Edward, Earl of Warwick, the son of the late George, Duke of Clarence (brother to Edward IV and Richard III), who was in fact safely under lock and key in the Tower of London. Martin Schwartz commanded 2,000 German mercenaries, who, along with some Irish troops, were led by Richard III's nephew the Earl of Lincoln. They landed in north Lincolnshire from the Low Countries on 4 June 1487 and marched into Yorkshire, before turning south to advance on Newark.

Meanwhile Henry VII was at Kenilworth, from where he moved his own forces through Leicestershire and towards Nottingham, passing through Bunny on 12 June and arriving in the county town two days later. Here the king attended the Corpus Christi Day service, probably in St Mary's church, before meeting up with Lord Strange's army, which had camped at Lenton. On Friday 15 June the combined army of 12,000 troops moved off to Radcliffe-on-Trent and commenced their advance up the Fosseway on the following day.

The opposing 8,000 Yorkist troops on that same date crossed the Trent, which appears to have been shallow in mid-summer, at a point near to Fiskerton. They then took up positions along a ridge that crossed the Fosseway between the villages of East Stoke and Elston. Here the Earl of Lincoln attacked the vanguard of the royal force led by the Earl of Oxford, knowing full well that with the arrival of the remainder of Henry's troops the Yorkists would be heavily outnumbered. Oxford was unprepared for this onslaught and his men suffered heavy casualties, and were only saved by the arrival of the main part of the Tudor army.

The tide now turned and it was the Yorkists who were on the run. Many of the Irish mercenaries tried to escape back across the Trent, but were cut down in their flight. Indeed the site of their massacre is still known as 'Bloody Gutter'. Altogether in the Battle of Stoke it is estimated that whereas the King lost something over two thousand dead, the rebels' total was nearer four thousand.

Amongst the local gentry who fought on the victorious side were

Dovecote on Clifton village green

52

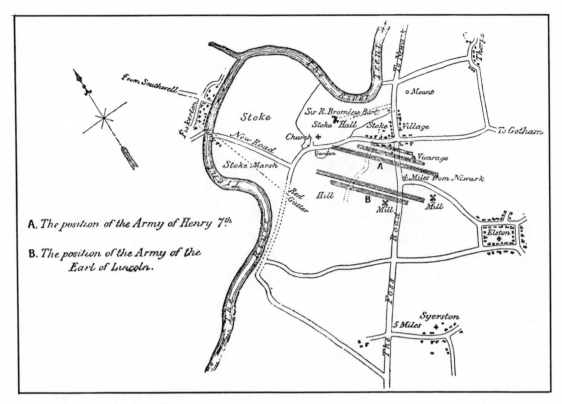

The Field of the Battle of Stoke

William Pierrepont, Edward Stanhope and Henry Willoughby, whilst in the ranks of the Yorkists the principal Nottinghamshire gentleman was Francis Lovel, who managed to swim back across the river only to die immured in his ancestral home of Minster Lovel in Oxfordshire.

Both the Earl of Lincoln and Schwartz lost their lives, whilst Lambert Simnel was taken prisoner and treated kindly by Henry VII, who sent him to the royal kitchens as a scullion.

Amazingly no English sovereign visited the county again until King James I passed through it during his slow progress from his old capital Edinburgh to his new capital London in 1603. So Queen Elizabeth I did *not* sleep in Nottinghamshire!

IX Monks, Nuns and Friars

Knob cross, Granby

It is difficult for us at the latter end of the 20th century in our secular British society to appreciate how important a role the monasteries, nunneries and friaries played in the life of the Middle Ages. They appeared throughout Nottinghamshire, although compared with neighbouring Lincolnshire their numbers were small. However, represented within the confines of Nottinghamshire were houses of most of the orders, the oldest of which were, of course, the Benedictines. Their sole representative in the county was founded by Roger de Busli at Blyth, near his castle at Tickhill, just over the Nottinghamshire border. This priory was a daughter house of the Abbey of Holy Trinity at Rouen (Roger's home town). When it was founded in 1088 its prime function was to pray for the souls of Roger and of that of the Queen, Matilda, wife of the Conqueror. It appears to have had an uneventful history. Its magnificent church still survives as the local parish church: an outstanding example of early Norman ecclesiastical architecture.

The lands of Ulf at Rufford passed to Gilbert de Ghent, Earl of Lincoln, after the Conquest. In 1446 Gilbert's descendant founded the county's only Cistercian house on the banks of the Rainworth Water, near the future town of Ollerton. Like other Cistercian houses following the reformed rules of St Bernard, its church was dedicated to the Blessed Virgin Mary.

As with the Cistercians, the Cluniacs were also a reformed offshoot of the Benedictines, and owed their allegiance to their mother church at Cluny in Burgundy. Eventually there were over 1,000 daughter houses scattered throughout Western Europe. The one at Lenton was established by William Peverel, dedicated to the Holy Trinity, and devoted to praying for the souls of King William I and his consort Matilda. Situated on the outskirts of Nottingham, the monastery thrived so well that, according to the *Valor Ecclesiasticus* drawn up in 1535 on the orders of Henry VIII's Vicar General Thomas Cromwell, its annual income was as high as £337. It must be remembered that since future taxation was likely to be based on such a figure, it is likely that the monks kept this as low as possible.

54

Welbeck Abbey on the fringe of Sherwood Forest, now a famous military academy, was originally the senior house of a group of seven established in England by a contemporary and friend of St Bernard, St Norbert at Prémentré in 1120. Based on the rules of St Augustine, this order sought out remote places and engaged in sheep farming. Welbeck was founded by Thomas de Flemmaugh (or possibly by his father, Richard) sometime at the beginning of the reign of Henry II. It had close links with Newhouse Abbey in Lincolnshire. Although the Premonstratensians were legally free from visitations by local bishops, they usually agreed that these could take place. At the time of the *Valor Ecclesiasticus* the value of this house, located within the manor of Cuckney, was as low as £14 per annum.

One of the nine Carthusian houses in this country (the order was originally founded by St Bruno at La Chartreuse) was located in the park of Nicholas de Cauntlow at Greasley, near the present mining community of Eastwood, and was known as the Priory of Beauvale. The original founder called it *pulchra vallis* – shades of Beaulieu in the New Forest! Indeed, it is only comparatively recently that this lovely area has been spoilt by modern coal mining techniques, although as long ago as 1397 the then prior granted a lease for the extraction of coal to William Monyash of nearby Cossall. The priory church was dedicated to the Holy Trinity. Because of its mineral wealth, this house flourished and was valued in the *Valor Ecclesiasticus* at £227 per annum.

By far the most numerous order in Nottinghamshire were the religious houses of those who followed the rule of St Augustine – the Austin Canons. Their most famous house must be Newstead, founded within the boundaries of Sherwood Forest, the church of which was dedicated to St Mary. This was a royal foundation by Henry II *c.*1170. Just before its dissolution it was valued at £167 per annum. Another nearby house of the Austins was the Priory of Felley, founded in 1156 by Ralph Britto of Annesley. Its value in Tudor times was £61 per annum. However, the first house of this order to be established in the shire was that at Worksop, founded in 1103 by William de Lovetot. The house at Shelford near the banks of the Trent was founded by one of Henry's friends, Ralph Haunsley. Perhaps its relative accessibility was the reason for its becoming the shrine for such 'relics' as the Virgin Mary's purification candle, her girdle and some of her milk. Shelford was therefore richer than some of the other Austin houses with an income in 1535 of £151 per annum. A fifth house of the Austin Canons was established in the 12th century by Ralph d'Eyncourt at Thurgarton as a memorial to Archbishop Thurstan of York. Although founded in 1187, those parts of the present parish church which date back to monastic times are no earlier than 1230, according to Pevsner.

Worksop priory gatehouse

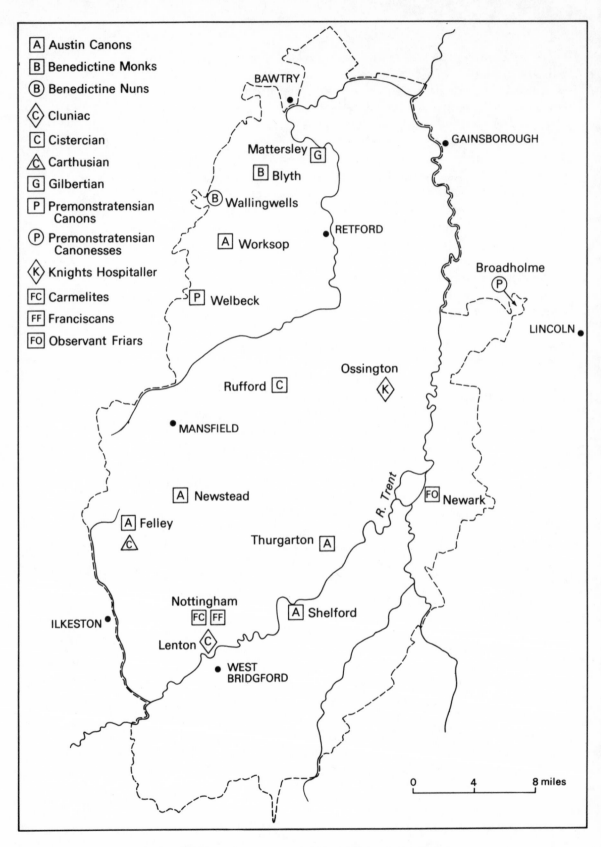

Key:

- [A] Austin Canons
- [B] Benedictine Monks
- (B) Benedictine Nuns
- (C) Cluniac
- [C] Cistercian
- (C) Carthusian
- [G] Gilbertian
- [P] Premonstratensian Canons
- (P) Premonstratensian Canonesses
- (K) Knights Hospitaller
- [FC] Carmelites
- [FF] Franciscans
- [FO] Observant Friars

BAWTRY

GAINSBOROUGH

Mattersley [G]

[B] Blyth

(B) Wallingwells

RETFORD

Broadholme (P)

[A] Worksop

[P] Welbeck

LINCOLN

Ossington (K)

Rufford [C]

MANSFIELD

[A] Newstead

FO] Newark

R. Trent

[A] Felley
(C)

Thurgarton [A]

Nottingham
[FC] [FF]

[A] Shelford

ILKESTON

Lenton (C)

WEST
BRIDGFORD

0   4   8 miles

Map 8. Monastic houses and friaries of Nottinghamshire.

The only native religious order was that founded by St Gilbert (1083-1189) at Sempringham, near Sleaford in Lincolnshire. Many of the Gilbertian houses were established in the saint's own county, but one was founded shortly before his death, in 1185, at Mattersey, on an island in the River Idle, by Ralph de Mattersey. This house's church was dedicated to St Helen – a popular cult figure in this region of England in the Middle Ages. A serious fire destroyed parts of this priory in 1279, and many of its charters and muniments. Henry IV granted the prior a weekly market and two annual fairs. The *Valor Ecclesiasticus* valued this convent at £39, made up of £9 per annum from land rents and £30 per annum from temporalities.

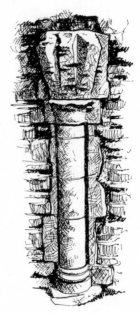

Column at Mattersey priory

The Benedictine nuns had a house at Wallingwells in the parish of Carlton-in-Lindrick, founded by Ralph of Chevrolcourt in his parklands during the troubled reign of Stephen. Its church became known as St Mary-of-the-Park. A visitation made in 1536 put the value of this house at £60 per annum.

At Broadholme in Harby parish on the borders of Lincolnshire stood one of only two houses for Premonstratensian canonesses in England (the other being at Orford, next to R.A.F. Binbrook in Lincolnshire). This was a late foundation in the reign of Edward II, whose consort Isabella became its patroness, giving to the house land worth eight marks (i.e. £5 6s. 8d.) in February 1327. Edward's mother, Queen Eleanor of Castile, had died in this parish in 1290, so obviously it had great significance for her only surviving son. At the time of the compilation of the *Valor Ecclesiasticus* its annual value had fallen to a mere £18.

During the Middle Ages there were only two friaries in the shire, and these were both situated in Nottingham. The Franciscans (alias Friars Minor or Grey Friars) were established there before 1230 on a site in the south-west corner of the Broadmarsh. In that year they were granted permission to build their chapel and six years later a quay on the local river. By 1256 they were wealthy enough to begin rebuilding their church in stone, using blocks from the royal quarry. Later they erected a preaching cross in what became known as Greyfriars Gate.

The Carmelite (or White) Friars were founded by their benefactor Reginald, Lord Grey of Wilton, *c*.1270, and were also assisted by Sir John Shirley. Their church (originally constructed from Sherwood oaks) was between Moothall Gate and St James's Lane, from which the names of Friar Lane and Friar Row derive (later re-named Beastmarket Hill).

A reformed sect of the Franciscans, the Observant Friars, made a very late appearance on the scene, being founded at Newark by Henry VII in 1507. Two years later he left them £200 in his will. Interestingly there were no houses of the Dominican (or Black) Friars in the county.

Seal from Observant friary at Newark

Likewise there were no preceptories of the Knights Templar in Nottinghamshire, although there was one belonging to the Knights Hospitaller, founded by Roger de Buron at Ossington in the 12th century. It became the source of litigation with Lenton Priory, which in 1208 was eventually decided in favour of the knights.

In addition to these 'regular' houses there were several other religious institutions which go under the generic title of 'hospitals'. These can be divided into two categories – leper houses (which included those suffering from other unseemly skin disorders) and those which cared for the aged poor.

In the former group came the Hospital of St Edmund at the northern end of Blyth, and a smaller house dedicated to St John the Evangelist at the southern extremity of this important village. Similarly, Bishop Alexander the Magnificent founded a leper (or 'lazar') house outside the town walls of Newark; this was dedicated to St Leonard – a popular choice for such establishments in medieval England. Another St Leonard's Hospital was founded (probably in Henry II's reign) outside the northern walls of Nottingham, whilst a third St Leonard's was established in Stoke by 1315. Although suppressed, with similar institutions, in the reign of Edward VI, they were revived by his half-sister Queen Mary I, only to be closed down by her half-sister Queen Elizabeth I. Dedications of such hospitals to St Mary Magdalen (herself regarded by her contemporaries as an outcast) were frequent, and are represented in Nottinghamshire by one outside Southwell in 'Esthappe feldes' by 1313.

The second category of medieval hospital, that for the aged poor, could be found throughout the county. Situated in that portion of Bawtry that was in Nottinghamshire, St Mary Magdalen's was established in Norman times and has continued in various guises into the present century (albeit converted into a carpenter's shop for a brief period from 1834 until 1839). Half way between Southwell and Nottingham was St Mary Magdalen's Hospital at 'Bradebusk' in Gonalston parish, founded by Willim de Heriz in the reign of Henry II. It too survived the Reformation. Thrice mayor of Nottingham John Plumtree founded the Hospital of the Annunciation of the Blessed Virgin Mary at Bridge End, later referred to as Plumtree's Hospital in Red Lion Square. By 1751 it still accommodated 13 widows. Other such hospitals in Nottingham were St Mary-at-the-West Bar and Holy Sepulchre. Finally, outside the town walls was the Hospital of St John the Baptist, where in 1241 the sisters and brothers are mentioned as wearing russet or black cloth habits, and one of the purposes of this house was to collect alms for the maintenance of Trent Bridge. Under the Poor Law Act of 1601 it became a secular poor house.

There were many close links between some of these houses and the county's secular clergy, the parish priests. This appears to have been especially so in the case of the Carthusians and the Observant Friars throughout the diocese of York (of which Nottinghamshire was a part in the Middle Ages), according to recent research by Dr. Claire Cross. For example, the Rev. Ralph Hedworth left £20 in his will to the Observants in Newark for obits (*annual* masses for the soul of the dead). The Rev. John Johnson (vicar of Mattersey) gave 6s. 8d. (33p) to his local prior for 'registering my name as a brother'. Dr. Cross has discovered that a quarter of the wills in the diocese in the 1530s showed their testators leaving money to the friaries. In other instances there were bequests to abbeys and priories, where their churches were the local place of worship (as in the cases of Blyth, Thurgarton and Worksop).

The alabaster industry benefited by the presence of local monastic houses, but unfortunately at their dissolution it is believed that such images and statuary were ground down to make plaster of Paris! Some valuable items were hidden from Cromwell's commissioners, and a superb medieval lectern, now in Southwell Minster, was discovered in the lake at Newstead Abbey 300 years after it had been hidden there by the monks.

After the Black Death (1348/9) many local landowners began to lease outlying granges from the monasteries and nunneries, so that at their dissolution the descendants of these lessees often became the new owners of such lands, retaining the former monastic servants as their own workforce. Perhaps this is one reason why Mary I did not attempt to disturb their occupancy of these lands when she mounted a Counter-Reformation in 1553?

The Reformation

In 1396 four Nottingham citizens, William Dynot (a former bailiff of the town), Richard Poucher, William Stoyour and Nicholas Taylor, were arrested and taken to London to be examined by the Archbishop of York to see whether they belonged to John Wycliffe's heretical Lollard sect. Six years later Robert Leycestre, a Nottingham Franciscan, was hanged at Tyburn for preaching that King Richard II was still alive.

These two apparently unconnected incidents are linked in as much as they demonstrate that there was an element of unrest within the Church at this period, which was beginning to challenge both the ecclesiastical and temporal establishments. Isolated examples they might be, but as the 15th century progressed the weaknesses of the Church in both its teachings and institutions became more evident.

During the Black Death of 1348/9 many clergy died. A. C. Wood has

Medieval church doorway

59

Dance of death panel, Newark church

estimated that 36.5 per cent of all livings in the county became vacant in 1349 alone due to this dreadful plague. However its incidence varied from 48.5 in the Newark deanery down to 25.5 in that of Bingham. A further, but less virulent, plague struck the area in 1369 carrying off 21.2 per cent of the priests in the Newark deanery, but only 8.5 per cent of those living in Bingham deanery. There must have been an even higher mortality rate amongst the brethren and sisters in the various monastic houses in Nottinghamshire; half of the monastic principals perished in 1349. Although the secular clergy did manage to get back to their normal numerical strength, their quality seems to have been debased. However, most convents never recovered from these mid-14th-century losses. In those places where they were able to recruit new blood, sometimes unworthy members entered their portals. Scandals resulted, like that in Nottingham in 1532 when the Carmelites' Prior, Richard Sherwood, had to obtain a royal pardon for having killed one of his friars, William Bacon, during a drunken brawl.

When Thomas Cromwell's commissioners visited the various monastic houses they occasionally discovered real scandals. More often they had to trump up charges in order to support a case for closing the houses, as happened at Shelford in 1536 when the commissioners Leigh and Layton accused three of the canons of 'unnatural sin' and another three of incontinence.

The heads of two Nottinghamshire houses were tried for high treason. Prior Nicholas Heath of Lenton was arrested in February 1538 after his house had been seized by attainder, thus effectively preventing the payment of pensions or other compensation to the brethren there. Convicted on the circumstantial evidence of a conversation with Hamlet Pentrich, Heath was executed that April, along with Ralph Swenson, one of his monks. Later another of the Lenton brethren, William Gylham, was hung, drawn and quartered in Nottingham, together with four of the lay brethren. Like other Carthusian leaders, who regarded themselves as guardians of the true Catholic faith, Prior Maurice Chauncers of Beauvale was arrested on 13 April 1535 and sent to the Tower of London. A week later he and two other Carthusian priors (of Axholme and London Charterhouse) were examined by Thomas Cromwell. Since they continued to dispute Henry VIII's claim to be Supreme Head of the Church in England they were executed with the usual barbarities at Tyburn on 4 May that year.

Not all the monastic houses in the county were dissolved in the same year. The first to close were Blyth, Broadholme, Felley, Rufford and Strelley in 1536. Another four were surrendered in 1538: Thurgarton (12 June), Welbeck (20 June), Mattersey (3 October) and Worksop (15

60

November). The remaining houses had purchased a reprieve in 1536, but this did not stop their closure in 1539: Beauvale (18 July), Newstead (21 July) and Wallingwells (12 December).

The fate of their buildings varied from site to site. At Blyth the magnificent late 11th-century church was stripped of its tower, choir and transepts, but the rest of this structure was handed over to the local inhabitants to use as their parish church. The same happened at Thurgarton and Worksop. Sir John Byron of Colwick purchased Newstead, retaining the west front of the priory church, whilst adapting many of the monastic buildings to become his new home, a home made famous by his descendant George, 6th Baron Byron, the poet. The site, together with that of Rufford Abbey, is now in the possession of Nottingham City Council. Other monasteries were completely demolished, although remains of Mattersey still stand gaunt on the banks of the Idle, guarded by the Department of the Environment.

Of the fate of the dispossessed brethren and sisters little is known. In some cases they were allowed to become secular parish priests. Thus brother Robert Armystede from Worksop Priory was placed in charge of Clarborough, whilst his fellow monk William Nott was presented to the living of Walkeringham. Two of the expelled brethren from Newstead, Christopher Matterson and Henry Tingker, were inducted to Walesby and Edwinstowe respectively, whilst Thomas Walless (Beauvale) became the priest at Adbolton. Because he had been co-operative with Cromwell's commissioners, Thomas Doncaster (Abbot of Rufford) was given the plum benefice of Rotherham.

The two Nottingham friaries were both suppressed on the same day – 5 February 1539. That same year the house of the Observant Friars in Appleton Gate, Newark, was also dissolved.

When the Dissolution and other aspects of the Henrician Reformation led first to the Lincolnshire Rising at the beginning of October 1536 and the subsequent Pilgrimage of Grace in Yorkshire later that month, the men of Nottinghamshire did not join in. On the contrary, many of them rallied to the standard of George Talbot, Earl of Shrewsbury, who gathered together the county's levies before marching on Lincoln, and thence to Blyth, en route to deal with the Yorkshire rebels, who had assembled at Pontefract.

However conformist Nottinghamshire appeared to be, there were, of course, those who were in favour of religious changes. The Dutchman Van Baller preached Lutheran doctrines at Worksop, whilst in the next decade John Lascells perished at Tyburn on 16 July 1546 for his Zwinglian beliefs, at the same time as that more famous heretic Anne Askew from Stallingborough in north Lincolnshire.

Some of the religious colleges and chantries were closed before 1545, but the remainder were suppressed under an Act of 1547. Their *raison d'être* had ceased once Edward VI's Parliament had repealed Henry VIII's Six Articles of faith, for now the belief in purgatory was abandoned. In Newark this involved 13 chantry priests based at the church of St Mary Magdalen. These were given varying pensions; Thomas Thorreton of the Holy Trinity received 100s. whilst William Gylbert was given the lesser sum of 71s. when he was deprived of his duties at St Catherine's chantry. Another town with a similar number of chantry priests had been Southwell. There were also three in St Mary's, Nottingham, and two stationed at St Nicholas's, Tuxford. Laxton had a chantry founded by Sir John Lexington in the mid-13th century.

Wild boar carving, Southwell Minster chapter house

Thomas Cranmer, Archbishop of Canterbury, was probably born at Aslockton, Nottinghamshire, in 1489. He was the 'Vicar of Bray' on the episcopal bench during the Reformation period and reflects the ambivalent attitude of the ordinary people of the county to the swings in government religious policy at this time.

X A Divided County

In 1567 the Shrievalties of Nottinghamshire and Derbyshire were divided after having been combined under one person since at least 1066. To this post had been added that of Lord Lieutenant, but not on a permanent basis until the 17th century. In Tudor times a nobleman would be appointed to this temporary office at times of crisis, such as happened in 1547 and again in 1549. In the former instance the Earl of Shrewsbury also held the Lord Lieutenancies of Cheshire, Lancashire, Shropshire and Yorkshire. In 1569, 700 Nottinghamshire men were recruited to put down the rebellion of the Northern Earls of Northumberland and Westmorland.

The leading families in the county provided many of the county and borough M.P.s in the 16th century – the Byrons, the Markhams, the Pierreponts and the Stanhopes. Amongst the *nouveaux riches* who now joined this select band were Denzil Holles (who represented East Retford in 1568) and Richard Whalley (County member in 1555). The Cavendishes, sons of that famous much-married Elizabethan lady, Bess of Hardwick, also joined their ranks. In 1616 Sir John Holles paid £10,000 for the barony of Haughton, and gave a further £5,000 eight years later for the vacant earldom of Clare. Likewise, Sir William Cavendish obtained from James I the viscountcy of Mansfield in 1620, followed by the earldom of Newcastle from the hands of Charles I in 1628. A third example is the progress of Philip Stanhope through the barony of Stanhope in 1616 to the earldom of Chesterfield 12 years later.

The English Civil War had many long- and short-term causes. Amongst the former were the anger over the imposition of extra-parliamentary taxation, resulting from the failure to summon a Parliament between 1629 and 1640, together with the sale of monopolies (i.e. the sole right to manufacture and/or sell a commodity) to royal favourites, which included the hated Robert Carr (James I's companion) and the Duke of Buckingham (that of Charles I). In the Isle of Axholme bordering on the northern extremity of Nottinghamshire the Isolonians had revolted against the forcible drainage of their fens (or carrs), under which they received back only one third of the land so 'reclaimed'.

Amongst the short-term causes of the War were the attempts to impose Ship Money (a tax normally paid by those living near coasts likely to be raided by pirates or enemy forces, and supposedly employed for boosting defences against such incursions) on inland counties such as Nottinghamshire. The imposition of the Arminian ('High Church') views of Archbishop William Laud of Canterbury upon a county that was rather moderate in its religious beliefs, along with the quick dissolution by Charles I of the 'Short Parliament' of 1640, followed by the attempted arrest of five members of its successor, the 'Long Parliament', by the king all helped to turn large sections of his subjects against his autocratic rule.

Hence on the eve of the Civil War Nottinghamshire seemed poised to continue its recent record of defending successive monarchs against their intended enemies. Yet the allegiance of the county proved to be far from a foregone conclusion. Whereas a petition to Parliament in 1641/2 was signed by gentry, clergy and the commons favouring episcopacy, a second such petition, with 1,500 signatures, expressing the contrary sentiment was delivered. A third petition, drawn up in the spring of 1642 and sent to Charles I at York, called on both sides to get together: amongst its signatories was the Mayor of Nottingham and several of the town's aldermen. A fourth petition stating a similar viewpoint and signed by 77 gentry was dispatched to Parliament. However, on 11 July of that year Charles I visited Newark to call personally on the townsfolk to remain loyal to him.

Nottingham Castle was already in ruins when John Leland visited it in 1540, and although Treasury warrants were issued in Elizabeth I's reign for its repair, this work had not been carried out by the time it passed into the hands of Francis, Earl of Rutland, in 1603. However, it was here that Charles I chose to raise his standard at six o'clock on the evening of 22 August 1642, having arrived in Nottingham three days earlier, accompanied by 800 horse. He made the Earl of Clare's property Thurland Hall his temporary headquarters. There he was joined by his nephews, the young German Princes Maurice and Rupert, who had been fighting in the Thirty Years War. The King's two eldest sons, Charles and James, also assembled there. However, the local response to this royal call to arms was disappointing, and only 300 enlisted under Charles's banner. Indeed, once the King had marched away to fight the indecisive battle of Edgehill, the town became a Parliamentary stronghold under George and John Hutchinson, who raised a force of 700 to defend it against any subsequent Royalist attack. John was a colonel and in June 1643 was appointed by Parliament Governor of the Castle.

Newark Castle

18a. Newstead Abbey.

18b. Kirkgate, Newark.

19. St Margaret's,
Owthorpe, restored *c*.1705.

20. The Cluniac priory church of SS Cuthbert and
Mary, Worksop, with its twin Norman towers.

21. The twin Norman towers of Southwell Minster, showing
also the Norman north transept and late 13th-century
Chapter House.

22. Sir Thomas Parkyn, Bart., designed Bunny Hall in the early 18th century to suit his own eccentric whims. This engraving shows the unusual gable end surmounted by a tower.

23. In its present form Holme Pierrepont Hall dates from 1790 and adjoins the perpendicular church of St Edmund.

24. Gateway, Clumber Park, showing the arms of the Duke of Newcastle.

25. Clumber Bridge, built in classical style over an artificial lake.

Support for the Royalist cause came from some of the local gentry. But whereas the Earl of Kingston was on Charles's side, his sons Francis and William Pierrepont adhered to Parliament. Henry Ireton, Oliver Cromwell's son-in-law and a Parliamentary commander, came from Attenborough to the south of Nottingham. To counterbalance this the recently elevated Marquess of Newcastle commanded one of the King's armies. The Earl of Chesterfield at Shelford held his manor house for the King, as did Lord Chaworth at Wiverton Hall.

Civil War coins from Newark

It was Newark and not Nottingham which was to become the Royalist headquarters in the East Midlands, being occupied on behalf of Charles by Sir John Digby as early as December 1642. Charles appointed the Scot Sir John Henderson to take charge of the garrison in the town, and he made his headquarters in the building in the Market Place that is still called the Governor's House. By February 1643 a narrow ditch and rampart had been constructed around Newark, just in time for the first of three Parliamentary sieges that commenced on 27th of that month. During three days of fierce fighting the Roundheads managed to penetrate these defences and get as far as Beaumond Cross and Northgate, before being repulsed and defeated.

On 16 June 1643 Queen Henrietta Maria with 4,500 troops arrived to reinforce the Newark garrison, having marched from their original landing point of Bridlington. And it was from Newark in the following September that a force of Cavaliers actually plundered Nottingham, holding Trent Bridge for a fortnight. Nevertheless, all attempts to capture the Castle itself failed. Not only did George Hutchinson reject the joint bribes of a title and £10,000 if he surrendered the garrison, but he threw back the retort, 'If my Lord would have that poor castle he must wade to it in blood'. Another effort by no less than 1,500 Royalists to storm it in January 1644 fared no better. In the interval between these two assaults Hutchinson had taken the precaution of demolishing the nearby parish church of St Nicholas, the tower of which made an ideal platform for cannon or snipers.

Another Parliamentary attack on Newark led by Major-General Sir John Meldrum was launched on 29 February 1644. The inhabitants had to endure a month of bombardment by cannons before Prince Rupert arrived at dawn on 20 March, leading 6,000 troops, having marched overnight from Bingham. His force defeated the Roundheads on Beacon Hill. Although the county witnessed no great battles on the scale of Marston Moor or Naseby, there were plenty of skirmishes, especially in the Newark area.

The King's soldiers were once again in the vicinity of Nottingham in April 1645, plundering West Bridgford and Wilford. Such forays were

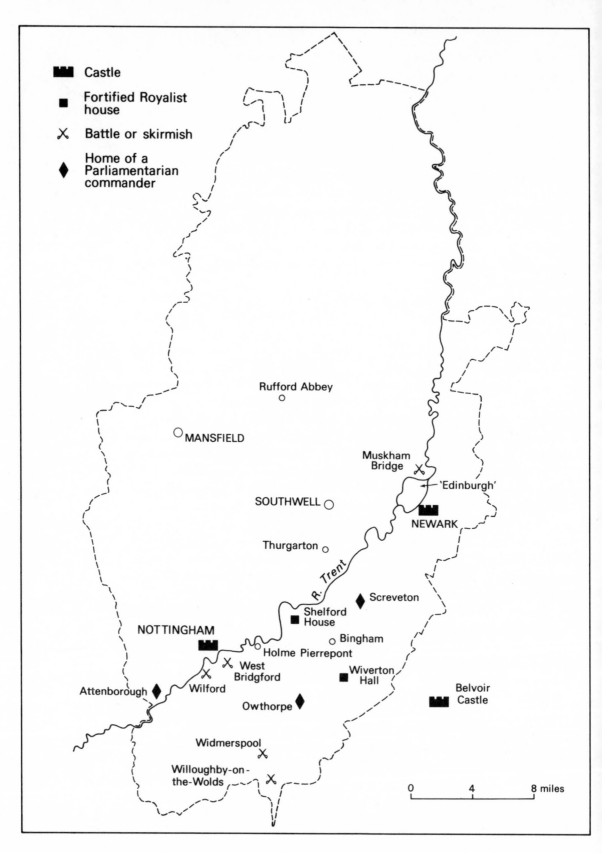

Map 9. Nottinghamshire in the Civil War.

Castle

Fortified Royalist house

Battle or skirmish

Home of a Parliamentarian commander

Rufford Abbey

MANSFIELD

Muskham Bridge

'Edinburgh'

SOUTHWELL

NEWARK

Thurgarton

R. Trent

Screveton

Shelford House

NOTTINGHAM

Bingham

Holme Pierrepont

West Bridgford

Wiverton Hall

Attenborough

Wilford

Belvoir Castle

Owthorpe

Widmerspool

Willoughby-on-the-Wolds

0   4   8 miles

even taking place after the disastrous defeat of the King's main army at Naseby on 14 June of that year. But in September Major-General Poyntz gathered a Parliamentary army at Nottingham for the final siege of Newark. On 3 November this force stormed Shelford House, putting its defenders to the sword, including its commander Colonel Philip Stanhope, who perished with 140 of his men. Afterwards the house was set on fire so that it might not be refortified later in the war. From Shelford, Poyntz turned south to attack Sir Robert Therrill's garrison at Wiverton Hall. Here discretion proved to be the better part of valour. After its surrender all but the gatehouse of this 15th-century moated manorhouse was levelled. Now Poyntz turned his attention to Belvoir Castle. Here no direct assault was possible, so its garrison had to be starved into submission – a task that was not achieved until the following February.

In the intervening period Charles and his nephew Prince Rupert had quarrelled at Newark over the latter's behaviour at the recent siege of Bristol, thus seriously undermining the Royalist cause. The Royalists had fortified Newark with a series of small square camps linked by a network of ramparts and trenches. These included the more massive earthworks known as the King's Sconce and the Queen's Sconce. An army of Scots under the Earl of Leven arrived near the town at Muskham Bridge on 26 November 1645, camping to the west of Newark on the island formed by the rivers Devon and Trent. This base they called Edinburgh! Leven's force consisted of 9,000 English and 7,000 of his native Scots. Within the defensive perimeter of Newark were up to 2,000 Cavaliers. Charles arrived at the *King's Head* (now called the *Saracen's Head*) in Southwell on 5 May 1646 disguised as a beardless priest. Here he formally surrendered himself to the Scots, apparently hoping for better treatment than if he had given himself up to the English. Next the King sent orders to his commander in Newark, Lord John Bellasis, to capitulate. This command was duly carried out on Friday 8 May, when Leven allowed the garrison to march out honourably. The orders were issued for the local villagers to level and fill up all the temporary fortifications, whilst the Parliamentary troops began the task of dismantling Newark Castle itself. Only the Queen's Sconce and the castle rampart at the end of this process remained for posterity. In the following March a similar order was given for Nottingham Castle. However, the final decree for its total obliteration was not given by the Council of State to Colonel Hutchinson until May 1651. He had completed this task by 7 July that year.

Newark was once more the focus of attention in the Second Civil War, when the Royalists advanced on it, arriving there on 4 July 1648. At

Saracens Head, *Southwell, where Charles I surrendered*

that time the main Parliamentary force in the county was stationed at Bingham. On the following day there was a skirmish between the two protagonists at Widmerspool – a precursor to the larger battle of Willoughby-on-the-Wolds, where the King's army was defeated and one of its senior officers, Colonel Gilbert Byron, captured. Marching towards the North to fight the Scots after their successes in South Wales, Oliver Cromwell's soldiers passed through Nottingham on 3 August 1648.

During the subsequent trial of Charles I two Nottinghamshire M.P.s sat on the special court and became regicides by appending their signatures to the royal death warrant. They were Colonel John Hutchinson (representing the county) and Gilbert Millington (Nottingham borough). Two other local regicides were Edward Whalley (of Screveton) and Henry Ireton. After the Restoration of Charles II they paid dearly for this action. Hutchinson, supported by the Royalist Lord Byron who testified to the Colonel's dislike of Cromwell, had his life spared and was able to retire to his estates at Owthorpe. However, unfortunately for him, the Northern Plot of 1663 led to apparently groundless suspicion that he was implicated in it, so he was rearrested. After being sent to the Tower he was incarcerated in Sandown Castle, Kent, where he subsequently died of natural causes on 11 September 1664. Millington was sentenced to life imprisonment on Jersey, where he died in 1666. Whalley escaped to America, where he lived in exile until his death in 1674. Ireton, who had died in 1651, because he was the Lord Protector's son-in-law, had his body exhumed, drawn on a hurdle through the streets of London on 30 January 1661 (the 12th anniversary of the execution of Charles I), and hung, drawn and quartered at Tyburn. Finally his head was placed in a prominent position at Westminster Hall, where it was still to be seen as late as 1685. A fifth Nottinghamshire Parliamentarian suffered the worst fate, for Colonel Francis Hacker was still alive when he endured the punishment of a traitor at Tyburn.

After the end of the monarchy in 1649, the King's Nottinghamshire supporters were permitted to repossess their lands upon the payment of a fine. The Earl of Chesterfield headed the shire's list, being required to pay the huge sum of £8,698 7s. 6d., followed by Sir Gervase Clifton with £7,625 3s. 8d. However, exceptions were made. On the one hand Royalist commanders like the Marquess of Newcastle and Sir John Byron were barred from repossession at any price; on the other the Earl of Kingston was excused a fine because his sons had given valiant service in the Parliamentary army.

During the Commonwealth period there were two Royalist plots that affected the county. The first took place on the night of Thursday 8

March 1655, when 300 conspirators met at the *New Inn* (near Rufford Abbey) with a cartload of weapons which had been conveyed from Thurgarton. But news arrived of the collapse of a similar plot in Yorkshire, so these arms were hastily dumped in a local pond and all quickly dispersed to their own homes. However, the ringleaders were rounded up and imprisoned. Partly as a result of such incidents Cromwell placed England under military rule for a short period. Major-General Edward Whalley was placed in charge of his native county, along with Derbyshire, Leicestershire, Lincolnshire and Warwickshire. The second plot was led by Richard, Lord Byron, who mustered 120 men near Sansom Wood, Sherwood, on 12 August 1659. The following day they marched towards Nottingham, diverted towards Derby and surrendered there on the 14th, there being little stomach left in the county for more civil strife.

There was to be one final entry into the county's Civil War annals. On 2 January 1660 General George Monck passed through Mansfield and Nottingham with his army en route from Scotland to London, where he began the process that resulted in the Restoration at the end of May.

XI Coal, Cotton and Ceramics

Coal mine horse gin

The first mention of coal mining in Nottinghamshire appears to be in a document of 1282 referring to Cossall where *minerarium de carbonious maris* (i.e. sea coal) was being extracted – probably by open cast methods. From the reign of Edward I also comes another reference to mining at Selston. Cossall was on land belonging to Newstead Abbey, whilst the Carthusians at Beauvale controlled not only the mining operations at Selston, but also at Kimberley and Newthorpe. In 1457 William Arnolde granted to the Prior of Beauvale rights to sink shafts, make drains (or adits/soughs) and take wood for 'punches' (joists) and 'proppes' for a term of 99 years at a peppercorn rent of one mark (i.e. 13s. 4d.) per annum. Two years later Lenton Priory obtained from Beauvale a certain proportion of their underground coal.

However, it was in the next century that the coal mining industry really took off. At Wollaton Sir Henry Willoughby was given permission by the Prior of Lenton to make a sough in order to extract coal. Demarcation disputes between the owners of the Wollaton mines and those of Strelley occurred. Nevertheless the huge profits made by the Willoughbys enabled Sir Hugh to finance and lead his famous expedition to Russia in the winter of 1553/4 and for Sir Francis to build the impressive mansion Wollaton Hall in 1580-88. As well as in Nottingham itself, there were ready markets in nearby Leicestershire and Lincolnshire, which were described as 'being veray bare and scarce conties of all maner of fuels'.

Sir Francis Willoughby also owned ironworks and experimented in the manufacture of glass. It has been estimated that the Wollaton pits produced at this date up to 20,000 tons of coal a year, which represented 40 per cent of the entire Nottinghamshire output. In Defoe's letter VIII, published in 1726 on his nationwide tour, he referred to the glass industry in these words: 'I think it is of late rather decayed'. It seems to have been replaced by an expansion of earthenware manufacture.

Defoe listed fine stone mugs, teapots and tea cups as being produced in Nottingham for the new vogue of tea drinking. The town had been a

70

ceramic centre since at least the 13th century when it was famous for its Green Glaze Ware, and in the early 18th century there were works such as those run by Morley, whose address was Mug-house Yard, Mug-house Lane, Beck Street. He specialised in brown mugs for use in public houses and also had made a general range of brown products known generically as Nottingham Ware since at least 1726. Amongst the items manufactured at other potteries were brown stoneware mugs in the form of a bust of Queen Anne, which was set between beefeaters, with dogs and a hare round the base and on the rim. A verse on the one made for William Marsh in 1729 read:

'On Banse downs a hair were found
Thatt led uss all a Smoaking Round'.

A similar one made for Edward Stark two years earlier showed hounds and a stag. A third example was roughly based on Hogarth's picture 'Midnight Conversation'.

Although William and Ann Lockett were still making salt-glazed stoneware in the town in 1755, much of the industry by that date had shifted over the county boundary into Derbyshire, and especially to Chesterfield.

Defoe remarked that there was very good liquor brewed in Nottingham and reckoned that their malt was the best in that part of England, being sold in Derby, Manchester, Cheshire and *even* (sic) in Yorkshire. Some of the cave cellars hollowed out of the Bunter Sandstone were used by the brewing industry, like the one excavated in 1966 under No. 8 Castle Gate where a well, a malt roasting oven with a firing pit and a large room for steeping the grain were uncovered. In other cases caves were employed for the storage of liquor under ideally cool conditions.

But it was perhaps Newark that could claim to be *the* brewing town of the county. The brewers there and in the nearby village of Fiskerton had to pay a 'tolsester' (a measure of beer) to their respective lords of the manor for the right to brew. For this purpose there was established in Newark a 'Tolsester Court of Brewers, Tippers and Huccsters', which met annually on the Monday after the feast of St Mary Magdalen (22 July) – the dedication of the parish church. No less an experienced traveller than Celia Fiennes wrote in 1695 that at Newark she had 'met with the strongest and best Nottingham ale that looked very pale but exceedingly clear'.

One cave excavated in the Broad Marsh area of Nottingham had apparently been dug out *c.*1270. At the beginning of the 16th century round and rectangular vats had been sunk into its floor when it became a tannery.

By the late 14th century a bell-founding industry had been established

Wollaton Hall

71

in Nottingham by the suitably named William Brasyer. In 1487 bell founder Richard Mellars became Mayor and his son Robert cast the bells for the great new steeple of St James's, Louth, in Lincolnshire, in 1510. This neighbouring county, which did not develop its own bell foundries, continued to purchase Nottingham bells from such later manufacturers as Henry Oldfield of Lister Gate. His family continued this craft for several generations until they sold out to Daniel Hedderley of Bellfounders' Yard in 1747 – a family which continued in this business until 1850. Another 18th-century Nottingham bell-founder was Tatham, who worked first in Castle Gate before transferring to new premises in Bridlesmith Gate.

Coal was not the only extractive industry in the county. There were rich beds of Keuper containing alabaster or gypsum either to be mined or quarried. Originally these were centred on Gotham and Orston – the latter place having gypsum described as 'the finest in the Kingdom'. This raw material took two forms. One consisted of nodular beds; the other was made up of spheroids known locally as 'balls' or 'bowls'. Whereas foliated gypsum was used mainly for tough, fire-resistant floors, the fibrous variety was ideal for carving into effigies. In the 14th century Peter the Mason of Nottingham became nationally renowned for his alabaster work, which included the reredos for the high altar in St George's Chapel, Windsor. His masterpiece was conveyed there in sections by 10 wagons, each pulled by an octet of horses. In 1414 the Abbot of Fécamp in Normandy sent a mission to Nottingham to buy unworked blocks of alabaster for shipping through Hull. Other blocks were exported further afield, to Ferrara in Italy and even to Iceland. A. C. Wood believes that many fine alabaster effigies found in local churches were carved in Nottingham, e.g. those of Sir Hugh de Willoughby (Willoughby-on-the-Wolds); Sir Henry Pierrepont (Holme Pierrepont) and Sir Robert Goushill (Hoveringham).

Defoe mentions framework knitting as Nottingham's principal industry, and indeed, by the time of his visit to the town, that part of the craft based in London had been transferred here due to lower overheads, lower wages and freedom from the tyranny of the regulations imposed by the Framework Knitters Company. Later they spread also to Mansfield, Sutton-in-Ashfield and Southwell. As the employment of paupers pushed down wage rates still further, the expression 'as poor as a stockinger' could be heard in the area by 1750. It was not until 1776 that they combined together and petitioned Parliament for a Bill to regulate their wages – a measure that failed due to pressure from their employers. When successive Nottingham M.P.s, Abel Smith and his brother Robert, prepared and presented a second Bill in 1779, rioting

Framework knitter's window, Calverton

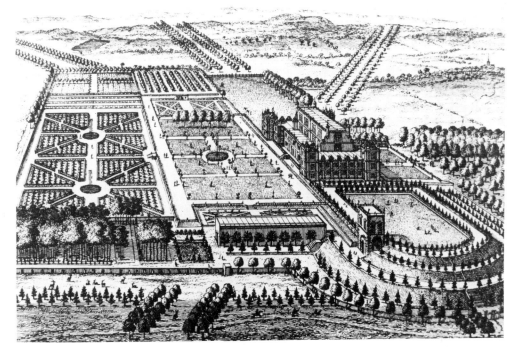

26. Sir Francis Willoughby commissioned Wollaton Hall in 1580. Its formal gardens are captured in this 1707 engraving.

27. Thoresby Hall was designed by Anthony Salvin for Earl Manners in the mid-Victorian period.

28. Nottingham's market place in 1849.

29. East Retford's town hall, built by Bellamy and Pearson in 1867, overlooks the market place.

30. Mansfield market place in 1987 with the modern stalls surrounding the 1849 monument to Lord George Bentinck.

31. Newark town hall was built of Mansfield stone in 1773 and faces onto the market place.

32. Ossington Coffee Tavern, Newark, built by Viscountess Ossington in 1882 to promote the cause of temperance.

33a.   Cave dwellings on Castle Rock, Nottingham.

33b.   East Retford market square.

and frame smashing greeted the defeat in the Commons again. The Riot Act was invoked and 300 specially sworn-in constables along with the cavalry were needed to restore order. When there was more rioting in 1787, frame smashing was designated a felony and a mandatory sentence of transportation attached to this offence.

Other branches of the textile industry were to be found in 18th-century Nottingham. In 1777 Robert Frost invented a square net for use by the lace industry in the manufacture of gloves, mitts, purses, shawls and wig foundations. There were at least forty machines devoted to the production of the last named product alone. In 1784 a Mr. Ingham introduced 'warp lace' to the town, and William Dawson established a factory in Turncalf Alley to manufacture it. Two years later John Rogers of Mansfield invented the fast-point net, which was soon being turned out on 50 frames. But these became obsolete in 1804 on the arrival of much finer yarn. In 1808 Joseph Page of Nottingham was able to produce the first piece of double-press print net using doubled fine yarn. Within two years there were as many as 15,000 employed in the local lace industry, working some 1,800 frames.

It was the arrival in 1768 of Richard Arkwright from his native Preston that put the Nottingham cotton industry on its feet. Partnering another Preston man, Smalley, he introduced his spinning frame at Hockley. This operated by means of rollers, four pairs of which acted by tooth and pinion. At first they had to be powered by horse gins, which proved to be rather expensive. Consequently in 1771 Arkwright moved to Cromford in Derbyshire where he could harness the water of the River Derwent to work his machinery.

James Hargreaves had arrived in Nottingham a year before Arkwright, establishing himself in premises in Wollaton Street. Here he carded, slubbed (twisted) and spun cotton. By 1794 there were eight cotton mills in Nottingham itself with a score of others spread through the county at Arnold, Basford, Cuckney, Fiskerton, Gamston, Langwith, Lowdham, Mansfield, Newark, Papplewick, Pleaseley, Retford, Southwell and Worksop. The plant at Papplewick was, in 1788, the first to utilise a Watts steam engine in the manufacture of cotton. By 1809 Mansfield had established itself as the second most important Nottinghamshire town in this particular industry with five mills, one of which employed 160 hands operating 2,400 spindles.

A large rise in bread prices after 1809, together with serious unemployment caused by Napoleon's Continental System (which involved a blockade of British goods) and the American Non-Intercourse Act, both of which had crippled the export trade, caused considerable unrest in the Nottingham area.

The Luddites were so-called because some of their public pronouncements were signed with the pseudonyms 'King Lud' or 'Ned Lud'. The movement was a spontaneous eruption of anger by handloom weavers (not only in Nottinghamshire, but also in Derbyshire, Lancashire, Leicestershire and Yorkshire) who feared that many of them would be made redundant by the advent of new machinery introduced into the hosiery and woollen-manufacturing industries.

The first Luddite violence was on 11 March 1811 when a protest meeting in Nottingham Market Place led to the destruction of about sixty frames. In the following week over a hundred more frames were destroyed in villages such as Bulwell, Lambley and Woodborough, as well as in the small town of Sutton-in-Ashfield. By the 29th of the month this vandalism had extended to Mansfield. On 13 April a reward of 100 guineas was offered after the wrecking of a further six frames at Bulwell. Thereafter, apart from one incident in the Ashfield area in July, there was a lull until November. On the 10th of that month there was a serious escalation of the trouble when the first fatality occurred. John Westley from Arnold was shot dead whilst (with accomplices) breaking into the house of a Mr. Hollingworth at Bulwell. Altogether in November between 160 and 190 frames were smashed, in addition to those broken during a daylight attack on an escorted cart load of such machines at Redhill. An accompanying campaign of rickburning against those opposing the Luddites happened on the 18th at Hucknall Torkard, Mansfield and Sneinton. The destruction and outrages continued right through December and on into 1812. New developments during this period included the extension of the Luddites' attentions to lace and silk frames, and the attacking of carriers. One from Sutton-in-Ashfield had all his cut-up hosiery goods destroyed on 25 January.

However, retribution was on the way and at the County Assizes on 17 March two Luddites were sentenced to 14 years' transportation and a further three to seven years each. But there were some acquittals at the same trial. Thereafter outbreaks of militancy were fewer and further between. In Nottingham there was trouble of a different kind that autumn with bread (11 September) and potato (3 November) riots. The year 1813 proved to be relatively peaceful, but there was an upsurge of Luddism in 1814, culminating in the murder of William Kilby and the attempted murder of Thomas Garton of New Basford. One of those involved, Samuel Bamford, lost his life.

At the Lent Assizes of 1815 one of the leading local Luddites, James Towle, was found 'Not Guilty' of breaking frames. However he was later executed for his part in a mill attack at Loughborough in Leicestershire. The last reported incident of Luddism in the county occurred at Bulwell on 2 November 1816.

XII Dissent of Many Kinds

Nottinghamshire seems to have had few important Roman Catholic adherents after the Elizabethan Church Settlement of 1559. In 1577 only 15 local names appeared on the recusant lists and by 1593 this figure had been reduced to fourteen. Neither was the Jesuit mission after 1580 successful in the county. In Watson's Plot of 1603 (to seize King James I and restore the Roman Catholic religion to England), only Sir Griffin Markham was involved and at the last moment he was reprieved and went into exile.

The Pilgrim Fathers, from a Scrooby inn sign

At the other end of the religious spectrum the Puritans were more in evidence. Several incumbents of this persuasion were dealt with in the ecclesiastical courts, e.g. Elias Okedeane of Greasley was presented in 1574 for refusing to wear a surplice, whilst Richard Clifton of Babworth was charged in 1593 with not making the sign of the cross nor of observing fast and holy days. Later this clergyman led a Puritan group based on Scrooby (near Blyth) which also included John Robinson (pastor from Sturton-le-Steeple), William Brewster (local postmaster) and the young William Bradford. They eventually went into exile in Holland after abortive attempts to flee first from Immingham and later from Scalp End on Boston Haven. Others to emigrate to this refuge of protestant dissent included John Smith (a Gainsborough Baptist leader, who also had pastoral oversight of North Nottinghamshire) and Thoms Helwys of Broxtowe Hall.

Yet during the archepiscopate of Richard Bancroft (1604-10), only four Nottinghamshire incumbents were deprived of their livings: Henry Aldrede (Marnham), Richard Clifton (Babworth), Robert Southworth (Headon) and Brian Vincent (Newark). Archbishop Richard Neile of York (1631-40) enforced his Canterbury colleague's Arminian rituals, which included genuflexion, standing for the creed and kneeling for communion. In January 1643 several more clergy were ejected, including Edward Bigland (Leake), Edmund Laycock (St Mary's, Nottingham), Joseph Rhodes (Haughton), Robert Thirlby (Clifton) and Frank Withington (West Bridgford). At the conclusion of the Civil War a further 20 clergy were removed from their parishes.

Mansfield Unitarian chapel

George Fox, a Mansfield shoemaker, began preaching at this time and amongst his early converts was Elizabeth Hooton of Skegby, who became the first woman preacher of the Society of Friends. In 1648 Fox was imprisoned following a disturbance in St Mary's church, Nottingham. After his release he moved to Mansfield Woodhouse, where he was placed in the stocks. However, these experiences did not deter him from returning to the county several times during the ensuing decade. By 1659 Quaker meetings in Newark were being broken up with violence. The persecution of this misunderstood sect depended largely on the attitudes of local Justices of the Peace. Some were harsh; others, like the Duke of Newcastle, lenient. Amongst those harassed was the historian of the county, Dr. Robert Thoroton.

The Five Mile Act of 1665 drove dissenters out of the towns like Mansfield to worship in the countryside, whilst under the Conventicles Act (1669) over 2,000 nonconformists were registered in Nottingham itself, including 500 Presbyterians, 200 Independents (who had numbered Oliver Cromwell amongst their members and were later known as Congregationalists) and 100 Quakers. Countywide there were 14 Presbyterian meetings (or conventicles), 11 Quaker, six Baptist and six Independent, making a total of thirty-seven. Three years later, under the Declaration of Indulgence, this total had increased by eight, all of which were made up of new meeting places of the Society of Friends. Under the Toleration Act of 1689, dissenters were given permission to build chapels. The earliest extant chapels that date back to this new building programme are the Quaker Meeting House at Blyth (1700) and that at Mansfield (1702). From a maximum of 51 in 1698, the number of dissenting chapels began to shrink during the reign of Queen Anne, so that there were only 18 of any size left by 1717, accommodating approximately 4,000 members. However, although in the first half of the 18th century some chapels (e.g. Calverton and Leake) were closed, others took their place (e.g. Arnold, Gamston, Misterton and North Collingham).

After the Restoration 38 Puritan clergy were ejected from their livings under the terms of the Act of Uniformity (1663). In some instances such clergy decided to conform to the Thirty-Nine Articles, but were given parishes elsewhere in the county. Thus Samuel Kendall left Widmerspool for Wollaton, whilst Thomas Salter was moved from Winthorpe to Caunton. Amongst those not so resettled were three Nottingham ministers – John Barrett (St Peter's), William Reynolds (St Mary's) and John Whitlock (St Mary's). After Monmouth's Rebellion in 1685 Reynolds and Whitlock were arrested on suspicion that they had some connection with that attempted rising. There were only three 'nonjurors' amongst the Nottinghamshire priests in 1689.

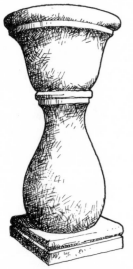

Georgian font, Kinoulton church

The Roman Catholic community within the county remained small and was largely restricted to a few squires and members of the aristocracy. So when the Catholic Bonnie Prince Charlie marched into England in 1745 to claim the throne on behalf of his father James, the Old Pretender, he found little support for his cause in Nottinghamshire. Indeed, on 1 October that year an association was formed in the county to fight the invader. The Duke of Kingston provided a troop of horse which was involved in a skirmish near Congleton and later pursued the fleeing Scots across the Border. Eventually, in the following April, they fought under 'Butcher' Cumberland at Culloden, after which Kingston's Horse was stationed at Fort Augustus for 'mopping up' in the Highlands, before returning to Nottingham to be demobilised on 5 September. However, it was not only the local Catholics who might wrongly be suspected of Jacobite sympathies, for the newly-recruited Methodists were also under a cloud during this troubled period!

The first Methodists in Nottingham appear to have been Howe and Rogers, who preached in the Market Place in 1740. When John Wesley himself paid the first of 28 visits to the town on 11 June 1741, he spoke in Howe's house. Towards the end of his ministry in 1777 Wesley noted, 'There is something in the people of this town which I cannot but much approve of'. The great little man visited Newark on half a dozen occasions, but only went to Retford and Worksop once each, and seems never to have preached in Mansfield. However he did have an especial affection for the society formed in the north Nottinghamshire village of Misterton on the edge of his native Isle of Axholme, and paid frequent visits to them as he journeyed to and from his home town of Epworth, where for a few years he was curate to his father Samuel. After meeting in members' houses for some years, permanent chapels began to be erected: the Octagon in Nottingham (1764), Newark (1776), Worksop (1780), Retford (1786) and finally Mansfield (1799).

Many schools started as church foundations. The earliest known in the county was that attached to Southwell Minster, which is known to have been in existence in 1238. After the college of canons there was dissolved in 1540, there was a short interregnum before a Grammar School was established in the town by an Act of Parliament passed in 1543. Also in existence in 1238 was Magnus Grammar School in Newark, although it only received this title after it had been refounded by Thomas Magnus in 1532. Under the terms of this bequest two priests were to be on its staff, one to teach grammar and the other singing. Every Friday both priests were to process with the scholars to the nearby parish church of St Mary Magdalene to attend the Jesus mass. Another medieval foundation was Nottingham Grammar School, mentioned in 1382, but

Magnus Grammar School, Newark

The Hawletts, Nottingham

possibly dating back to 1137. This was refounded by Sir Thomas Lovell and Agnes Meller in 1512. East Retford Grammar School may have been functioning as early as 1399; in 1518 it received a benefaction from Thomas Gunthorpe, the vicar of Babworth.

Although the religious motives for doing such good works for the salvation of the soul officially came to an end with the succession of Elizabeth I, new schools continued to be established. Thus in 1561 that sovereign was presented with a petition for a 'free Grammar School . . . in the town of Mansfield for instruction of boys and youths in grammar'. However not all such schools taught Latin and Greek: All Saints Grammar School, founded in Elston in 1615, never offered more than an elementary curriculum. Several other village schools were established in the 17th century, including those at Ruddington (1641), Sutton-in-Ashfield (1669), West Drayton (1688), South Leverton (1691) and Morton (1695). At Misson the schoolroom was built in the churchyard in 1693, emphasising the continuing links between religion and education. The turn of the century saw two contrasting schools: at Bunny in 1700, the Parkyn family provided the money for a school and proclaimed its objectives along the string course on the exterior of the building: *Scientia non habet inimicum nisi ignorantem – Disce et Discede – Nemo hinc egrediatur ignarus Arithmetices*. Sir Thomas Parkyn himself designed the building in an Italian style. At Harworth it was the Baptists who provided the new school.

As well as the foundation of new establishments in the towns (e.g. Worksop, 1628; the Blue Coat School, Nottingham, 1706; Brunt's School, Mansfield, 1706; East Retford, 1727; Nottingham High Pavement by the Society of Protestant Dissenters, 1788), many villages gained similarly, from Walkeringham (1719) in the north to Sutton Bonnington (1718) in the south, from Oxton (1783) in the west to Beckingham (1731) in the east. So by 1800 there were already 66 Nottinghamshire parishes that had their own school.

In 1810 two new religious bodies began to fill the remaining gaps or to replace worn-down schools. Joseph Lancaster's British and Foreign Schools Society opened one such in a disused cotton mill at Broad Marsh, Nottingham, whilst the Rev. Andrew Bell's National Society for the Education of the Poor in the Principles of the Church of England started a school in a former *chapel* in High Cross Street. There were already Sunday Schools in the county; the first was opened by William Hall at Mansfield Woodhouse in 1781. It has been estimated that by 1802 there were no less than 1,700 children attending such institutions in Nottingham alone.

Likewise, in some instances the Church was responsible for the pro-

Gazebo, Beckingham

vision of public libraries and reading societies in this period. The Rev. William Standfast (rector of Clifton) deposited his books at the Blue Coat School, Nottingham, in 1744 to form the nucleus of such a library.

Dovecote holes from a barn in
South Wheatley

XIII From Stages to Steam

Old toll house, Littleborough

Smithy, Carlton-on-Trent

Since Roman times roads between towns like Newark and Bingham had not been relaid. Other parts of the county had never had the benefit of such ancient highways, so by the 18th century long distance travel was well nigh impossible particularly during periods of bad weather. For example, during the winter of 1763/4 no coal could be transported from Belper to Nottingham because of deteriorating road conditions. Again, the sandy nature of the soil between the towns of Worksop and Warsop made travel very trying when it was wet. Yet in a few places help was at hand. In 1725/6 that section of the Great North Road between Grantham and Little Drayton (including the section through Newark) had been turnpiked, and many passengers and waggoners must have been only too pleased to pay tolls in order to move faster over a smoother surface. A decade later in 1737/8 the Nottingham to Loughborough road (the present A60) was given similar treatment, whilst its northern extension to Mansfield was taken over by a turnpike trust in 1787. Meanwhile the Great North Road between Markham Moor and Barnby Moor had been diverted in 1765/6 to go via the growing town of East Retford.

All these road improvements had their effect on stage coaches. In 1760 a so-called 'Flying Machine' had been introduced on the service from Sheffield to London via Nottingham, taking three days for the journey – a time that was cut to just one day by 1800. Then in August 1785 John Palmer introduced his first Royal Mail coach, which competed very favourably with the existing stage coaches. However, the peak of this competition was not reached until the 1830s – the very decade that saw the construction of the first main railway lines into London and the drawing up of plans to bring this newer, faster form of transport into Nottinghamshire as well. In 1836 only two named London-based stage coaches actually terminated in Nottingham. W. Chaplin & Company, operating from the *Swan With Two Necks* in Lad Lane, London, worked the 124-mile route employing his 'The Times' for the morning departure and 'The Commercial' for the evening run. Four vehicles were required to keep this service going, each seating four passengers inside and eight

80

outside. The daylight journey took 14 hours 45 minutes, whilst the overnight trip was scheduled to last 18 hours 30 minutes. Other through coaches calling in at Nottingham included 'The Express' operated by E. Sherman & Company out of the *Bull and Mouth* (originally called the *Boulogne Mouth*) in St Martin-Le-Grand in London, with a final destination in Leeds. J. Francis & Company working out of the *Belle Sauvage* (named after Princess Pocohontes) on Ludgate Hill also ran on this route with their 'The Courier', and this particular coach operated via Mansfield as well as Nottingham. However Newark and Retford, lying on the Great North Road, were better served. Here, if they wanted to travel to London, they had a choice; they could go by 'The Union' or 'The Rockingham' (from Leeds), 'The Lord Wellington' (Newcastle-upon-Tyne) or 'The Royal Express' and 'The Highflyer' (York).

With the advent of Royal Mail coaches the choice became even wider. The London to Thurso mail, which had the longest route of all, passed daily through Newark and Barnby Moor on its four-day journey to the other end of this island, whilst the London to Glasgow mail travelled via Newark, Ollerton and Worksop. Both routes in 1836 were operated under licence by E. Sherman & Company. Nottingham itself was served by two similar routes. B. W. Horne & Company operated the London to Halifax service for the Post Office, which departed from the *Golden Cross* at Charing Cross at 7.30 p.m. each evening, reaching Nottingham via Leicester at 6.50 a.m. The return journey began at 6.08 p.m., arriving in the capital at 7.02 next morning. The two vehicles employed on this route passed each other at Newport Pagnell in Buckinghamshire. The other Royal Mail service that passed through Nottingham was the one between London and Leeds, worked under licence by E. Sherman and Company. Since this made a detour through Oakham it did not arrive until 9.11 a.m., before carrying on through Mansfield.

In 1836 there were also three cross-country Royal Mail routes that passed through Nottinghamshire: Louth to Sheffield, Birmingham to Sheffield, and Grantham to Nottingham. Likewise, there had grown up a network of cross-country stages, many of which were operated by local proprietors instead of by the large London-based firms. Altogether in 1836 there were 27 of these criss-crossing the county, varying in length from local ones such as those between Nottingham and Heanor (10 miles) and Nottingham and Ilkeston (8 miles) to long-distance routes such as Nottingham to Manchester (70 miles) and Nottingham to Barton-upon-Humber for the Hull ferry (73 miles). In all, Nottingham city had 16 such routes, Newark eight, Mansfield and Worksop four apiece. The usual type of coach used on these services sat four inside and 11 on the roof, although there were many variations, with outside

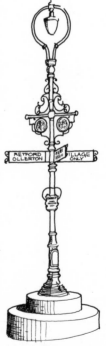

Combined lamp and guide post, Tuxford

Chesterfield canal bridge

numbers as low as five, and one that had room for just four inside passengers and none on the roof.

In December 1772 an Act of Parliament was passed for the building of two large locks on the River Trent near Newark. These were opened with great local celebration in the following October. In 1793 the engineers William Jessop and Robert Whitworth surveyed 71 miles of the Trent from Cavendish Bridge down to Gainsborough, discovering that, whereas for 65 of these miles there was a minimum depth of three feet (1 m.), in the remaining stretches there were up to seventy shallows. This was particularly true near the confluence with the Soar. Amongst their recommendations were the construction of a lock at Thrumpton, a second lock and cut at Beeston, and a similar combination of works at Holme Pierrepont. All this was estimated to cost £12,776. Next year an Act of Parliament enabled these improvements to be carried out, giving the river a minimum depth of 2 ft. 6 in. (0.76 m.), and thus allowing the passage of barges of dimensions 85 ft. 9 in. (26 m.) by 14 ft. 9 in. (4.5 m.) throughout the county's section of the Trent. Within five years there were some one hundred and forty of these craft plying their trade, and by 1817 a steam packet service was operating between Nottingham and Gainsborough. The traffic down the river consisted of beer kegs, Cheshire cheese, coal, copper, ironstone, lead, pottery and salt, whilst upstream went flax, hemp, iron ore from Sweden, malt and Norwegian timber.

Even before the first of the above improvements took place, work had begun on the Chesterfield Canal, which left the Trent at West Stockwith. This waterway passed across the northernmost part of Nottinghamshire, before entering Derbyshire near Worksop. Because of the terrain on this route it was necessary to include no less than 65 locks over its 46-mile length. Each of these locks measured some 72 ft. (22 m.) by 7 ft. (2.1 m.). It was opened in 1777; in the same year construction work started on the Erewash Canal along the western boundary of Nottinghamshire. This took only two years to complete, was $11\frac{3}{4}$ miles long and had 14 locks. This waterway was to become vital in the further expansion of the coal industry in this area.

Between 1792 and 1796 work continued on the Nottingham Canal, linking the Trent with the existing Cromford Canal at Langley Mill. This was $14\frac{3}{4}$ miles long and had 20 locks. To this main canal over the next half century were added six branches, none of them longer than $1\frac{5}{8}$ miles and half of them privately owned: Poplar Brewery (c. 1794), Robinettes (1796), Bilborough (1799), Greasley (1800), Morves (c. 1836) and Westcroft (1842).

Canal boat, Chester-field canal

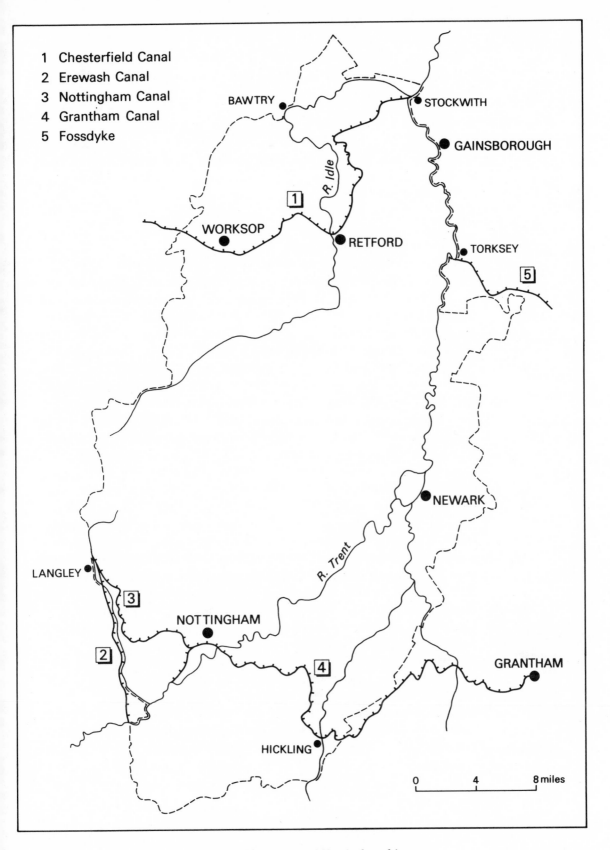

1 Chesterfield Canal
2 Erewash Canal
3 Nottingham Canal
4 Grantham Canal
5 Fossdyke

BAWTRY

STOCKWITH

GAINSBOROUGH

R. Idle

1

WORKSOP

RETFORD

TORKSEY

5

LANGLEY

3

R. Trent

NEWARK

NOTTINGHAM

2

4

GRANTHAM

HICKLING

0   4   8 miles

Map 10. The Canals of Nottinghamshire.

However, the greatest achievement, because of its length and the geological difficulties encountered in its construction, was the Grantham Canal, built between 1793 and 1797, which joined the Lincolnshire market town and the Trent near West Bridgford. It meandered through the Vale of Belvoir and needed reservoirs to prevent the water level from dropping. It had 18 locks. A ballad was composed in its honour, to be sung to a popular tune of the times, 'The Roast Beef of Old England'. The penultimate verse read:

> Whilst politics trouble the heads of the great,
> We'll leave them alone to the wise ones of fate,
> For Boats, Locks and Bridges our care does await,
> To finish our new Navigation,
> To finish the Grantham Canal.

Some of these canals were subsequently purchased by rival railway companies: The Manchester & Lincolnshire Union Railway Co. bought the Chesterfield Canal in 1847, whilst the Ambergate Railway Co. acquired the Grantham Canal in October 1854 and the following year the Nottingham Canal.

The first of these canals to be closed to traffic was the Nottingham in 1928 (being abandoned in 1937). Next to go was the Grantham (abandoned in 1936). The Erewash continued until 1952 (being abandoned in 1962). The 3,102 yard (2,838 m.) Norwood to Worksop tunnel on the Chesterfield Canal had been closed *c.* 1908, and the section beyond this was abandoned in 1962, leaving only the Worksop to Trent portion still in use.

The first 'railroad' in Nottinghamshire antedated the first stage coaches by half a century, for it was in 1604 that the Wollaton Railway was laid down between Wollaton Lane and Strelley Pits, being, perhaps, England's first such industrial line. However, it was not until the early years of the 19th century that any more of these short mineral railways were constructed. In 1805 the Giltbrook Bend, Greasley to Watnell Hall & Wool Pit line was built, a mile-and-a-quarter of track to link canal and coal-mine – a purpose that was behind the majority of such small lines. In 1817 several were opened, including those that linked Brinsley Wharf and North Brinsley colliery (three-and-a-quarter miles), Langley Bridge and Brinsley colliery (two miles), and Robinettes Arm and 'Old Engine' (only half a mile).

When the passenger train made its début in the county some two decades later, Robin Leleux reminds us: 'from the beginning of trunk railway development, Nottingham effectively was on a branch line while Leicester was on a main line'. This is the key to understanding the early and subsequent development of the complicated and, in places, dense

Bollard on the Trent Navigation

network of lines that was created between 1836 and the end of the century.

Trent ferry boat

In 1836 a Bill was presented before Parliament for two lines for the newly formed Midland Counties Railway Company. The first of these was to connect Nottingham with Derby – a distance of 15½ miles. This was duly constructed and opened with great ceremony on 30 May 1839 amidst the pealing of church bells and the playing of military music. As each of the four inaugural trains departed from Derby, the National Anthem was played. When the official guests returned to Derby an hour later, safe and sound, they were duly wined and dined in style to the usual accompaniment of self-congratulatory speeches. A top speed of 40 m.p.h. was recorded and this surely must have impressed those who experienced it. The public service commenced the following Tuesday, 4 June, with four return journeys per day and trains calling at the intermediate stations of Beeston, Long Eaton, Breaston and Burrewash. The fares charged for the complete distance were 4s. (first class) and 2s. 6d. (second class).

The second line authorised in the Midland Counties 1836 Act was from the fictional place called 'Trent' (located in Long Eaton parish) to Leicester and Rugby. The first section of this line, that between Trent and Leicester, was opened on 4 May 1840, whilst the remainder down to Rugby came into use on 30 June that same year; Trent station itself did not become operational until 1 May 1862!

In 1844 the Midlands Counties Railway Company merged with two others to form the Midland Railway Company under the aegis of 'Railway King' George Hudson. One of the first projects undertaken by this enlarged operator was to build a line from Nottingham along the Trent valley to Newark and from thence to Lincoln. Since there were no steep gradients to encounter, the work took just eight months to complete; the line opened on 3 August 1846. The original Nottingham terminus was in Carrington Street, but a new terminus in Station Street took over with effect from 22 May 1848, and the Carrington Street premises became a goods depot. The year 1848 also saw the Midland applying for parliamentary approval for another route to link Nottingham to Mansfield; with eight intermediate stations, this line opened to traffic on 9 October 1849, almost exactly a year after the Midland branch to Pinxton started operations.

The grandiose plan of the Ambergate, Nottingham, Boston & Eastern Junction Railway Company to run from Derbyshire to Kings Lynn was eventually truncated to become the comparatively short, flat stretch of line between Nottingham and Grantham, which opened on 15 July 1850 with four trains per day in each direction. Even this proved to be too ambitious, for within a fortnight the service offered was drastically reduced to a single passenger train each way! Since the Great Northern Railway Company was driving its so-called 'Towns Line' northwards towards Grantham and wanted to obtain a foothold in Nottinghamshire, it approached the Ambergate Company with a view to joining forces. This so frightened the Midland Railway that on 1 August 1852 they took drastic steps to foil this threat to their Nottingham to London service. As a G.N.R. locomotive passed Colwick on its way into the city, an M.R. engine trailed it. Spectators later described the ensuing chase as being rather like an elephant hunt! 'The G.N.R. driver made a sporting charge at his captors in a hopeless attempt to get away, but he was evicted from his steed which was borne away in triumph and locked in a shed. As a final indignity, the rails were removed and there the locomotive stayed for seven months', according to R. Leleux. This was by no means an isolated incident, for most regions had similar tales to tell at the close of the period known as the 'Railway Mania'. Eventually, on 2 April 1855, the Ambergate Railway was leased to the G.N.R. for 999 years. As a corollary to this compromise, a new station for the Nottingham to Grantham line was built in London Road, as well as the laying down of tracks that ran parallel with those of the M.R. between Colwick and the city centre.

The 'Towns Line' out of Kings Cross had been delayed by difficulties encountered to the south of Grantham in digging the Stoke Summit tunnel, so trains did not start running on this section until 1 August 1852, when Northgate Station, Newark and another at Retford made London more accessible to Nottinghamshire residents. The workshops for this main line might well have flourished at Newark had not the Duke of Newcastle objected, thus forcing the G.N.R. to establish them at Doncaster instead.

While all this was going on in the south of the county, at its northern end the Manchester, Sheffield & Lincolnshire Railway Company was driving a line from Woodhouse Junction through Worksop to Retford and on to Gainsborough. This received its first passengers on 16 July 1849. A branch line from Clarborough Junction crossed the Trent near Torksey and joined up with the G.N.R. line from Lincoln to Gainsborough at Sykes Junction near Saxilby. Since it was in the interests of both companies to engage in through traffic, this branch was a joint effort.

The latter half of the 19th century was a time both for consolidation and for opening an ever more complex and interwoven network of branch lines, many of them as a result of the demands of local industrialists, especially of coal owners. However, there were some new lines that

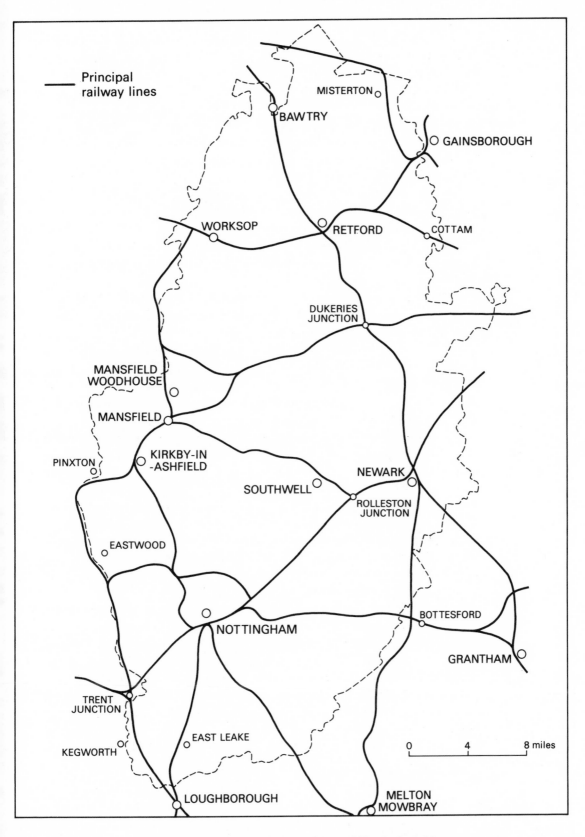

Principal railway lines

MISTERTON

BAWTRY

GAINSBOROUGH

WORKSOP

RETFORD

COTTAM

DUKERIES JUNCTION

MANSFIELD WOODHOUSE

MANSFIELD

PINXTON

KIRKBY-IN -ASHFIELD

SOUTHWELL

NEWARK

ROLLESTON JUNCTION

EASTWOOD

BOTTESFORD

NOTTINGHAM

GRANTHAM

TRENT JUNCTION

KEGWORTH

EAST LEAKE

LOUGHBOROUGH

MELTON MOWBRAY

0   4   8 miles

Map 11. The principal Railway Lines of Nottinghamshire.

aimed principally at linking all towns, however small they might be. As early as 1847 a two-and-a-half mile single track was laid down between Rolleston Junction (on the Nottingham to Newark line) and Southwell (later to be promoted to a cathedral city). But this proved to be so in advance of demand that by 1853 the service had been reduced to one *horse-drawn* train per week! Yet nearly twenty years later, in April 1871, this branch was improving so fast that it was extended beyond Southwell to Mansfield, and the wooden station in Southwell was replaced by a stone structure.

On the eastern side of the county a branch was authorised in 1873 from Newark down to Bottesford West Junction (on the Nottingham to Grantham line), and this was duly commissioned on 1 July 1878. The following year a southerly extension of this branch took travellers across the Vale of Belvoir, through Melton Mowbray down to Market Harborough on the L.N.W.R. main line. Contemporary with this development was the M.R. line from Nottingham to Melton Mowbray, thus connecting with that company's long-established service to Stamford and Peterborough. Once a connecting line between Manton (on the M.R,'s Melton Mowbray to Peterborough route) and Glendon Junction (on that company's Wellingborough to Leicester line) had been built, expresses could cover the distance from St Pancras to Nottingham in two-and-a-quarter hours, cutting time because of the route's easy gradients. This new service began on 1 June 1880.

The Nottingham Suburban Railway began to serve the city's growing commuter villages in 1889. At the start only horse-drawn buses and carriers' carts competed with these new trains, but once Nottingham City's own electric trams extended to these north-eastern suburbs then the rail route became unprofitable and the service ceased on 1 July 1916 – the first of many 20th-century line closures within the county. Many other lines on the western fringe of Nottingham had been built to serve coal mines: for example, Nottingham to Pinxton (1 August 1876), Nottingham to Burton-on-Trent (1 April 1878) and Nottingham to Newstead (2 October 1882).

It was in 1893 that an Act authorised the M.S. & L.R. to build a connecting line south of Nottingham to join up with the Metropolitan Railway line from Marylebone, thus establishing the Great Central Railway Company. Massive construction works were necessary at the Nottingham end of this new line. For example, the London Road High Level station stood near such engineering achievements as a 2,500 yard long tunnel, a mile-long viaduct and the cutting away of 600,000 cubic yards of sandstone rock. Then there was the Victoria Station, appropriately opened on the Queen's 81st birthday (24 May 1900). This stood on a 13-acre site cleared of 1,300 squalid houses. This project alone cost £1,000,000. The station boasted no less than 12 platforms from which travellers could board trains for destinations as far apart as Aberdeen and Penzance.

Crest on Wilford Bridge

XIV Nottingham

Victorian street lamp,
Trent Bridge

In medieval Nottingham various crafts and trades were gathered together in particular streets, as was common in other towns at that period. For example, there were Fishergate, Fletchergate (where the fleshers or butchers worked), Listergate (dyers), Pilchergate (furriers), Smith Row and Wheelergate. Gilds of craftsmen were also established at an early date; in 1155 the dyers paid £2 per annum for the right to found such an organisation to regulate their members and their craft. Above all, the River Trent gave the town its importance, for not only was it the main avenue for the moving of raw materials and finished products, but it was an additional source of income. Tolls were charged on traffic going to and from towns further upstream.

To become a burgess of the town a residential qualification of one year and one day was necessary. However, Nottingham remained divided between the old pre-Conquest borough and that established by its side around the Castle after 1066. A charter of 1284 provided that, if either of the separate boroughs was unable to find a bailiff (a chief officer, who was the King's representative in a town), then the other could choose both of them for that year.

A later charter of 1399 added four Justices of the Peace (who were also responsible for artificers and labourers) to the town's hierarchy, along with a mayor and a recorder. However, in 1413 it seems likely that there were as few as 49 burgesses who were entitled to participate in the election of the mayor and bailiffs. By the middle of that century a council of 12 was also elected to help in the government of the town.

But the great stride forward came in 1448 when Henry VI raised Nottingham to county status. This meant that the two bailiffs were now elevated to the posts of Sheriff, able to hold monthly county courts. Seven aldermen (one of whom would hold the office of Mayor) were elected, holding this honour for life, provided they remained in Nottingham and were of good behaviour. These aldermen additionally acted as Justices of the Peace.

By 1606 the burgesses were appealing to the Privy Council over the oligarchy who were then running the town, and that august body decreed that in future a council of 24 should take over the running of Nottingham. Three-quarters of these should be 'of the clothing', but at least six commoners were to be included, being chosen by the Mayor and burgesses at a special meeting. Whether in the end the abuses complained of were rectified by such a shake-up in local government seems uncertain. In that same year the Earl of Shrewsbury became the last life-holder of the High Stewardship of Nottingham. Another innovation was the appointment of non-lawyers to the post of Recorder (e.g. John, Earl of Clare, in 1642; Henry Pierrepont, Marquis of Dorchester, in 1669).

After the Restoration the ruined castle site passed into the hands of the Duke of Buckingham (one of the members of the famous Cabal), who in his turn sold it to the Duke of Newcastle in 1674. He set about clearing the top of the great rock ready for the erection of a fine mansion. But the great general of the Civil War died two years later at the age of 83, leaving his son Henry to complete the work. John Holles, 4th Earl of Clare, married Henry's daughter Elizabeth and was himself created 3rd Duke of Newcastle in 1694, at which time he was deemed to be the wealthiest Englishman alive.

'Wrestling baronet',
Bunny church

In 1682 Charles II had presented Nottingham with a new charter, having ordered the surrender of all the old ones. This was purely a political move aimed at excluding the Whigs from office. Nevertheless, a few years later, after the abdication of his brother James II during the Glorious Revolution, these old documents were returned to the town in part payment for the support given by Nottingham to William III directly he had landed in his bid to oust James II from power. The townsfolk were smarting from the rough treatment which they had received at the hands of Lord Dumbarton's Regiment. James's daughter, the Princess Anne, fled to Nottingham on 2 December 1688, and was escorted to Oxford, where she was reunited with her husband, Prince George of Denmark. In 1695 William III visited the town – the last sovereign to do so until Queen Victoria in 1843.

Like many other English towns at this time, Nottingham was being rebuilt in brick and stone: partly because this was now fashionable, partly because its chief citizens were rich enough to do so, and partly because of the risk of serious fires from timber-framed buildings, as had happened in London, Northampton, Southwold and elsewhere. Much of the brick used was made from earth dug on Mapperley Plains. Nottingham's growing wealth was due to the expansion of its local industries and the proximity of the coalfield (see chapter XI above). Thomas Smith of Tithby, a mercer, became the town's first modern banker, founding an institution that was to survive for many years after his death in 1699. During the 17th and 18th centuries the richer element

Lord Byron's town house,
Nottingham

Upton Hall, now the British Horological Institute

in Nottingham society began to erect town mansions with formal gardens around the Lace Market, and this gave Nottingham the nickname of the 'Garden Town'. When, in 1677, the much-travelled Celia Fiennes visited the town she wrote that Nottingham was 'the neatest town I have seen . . . delicate, large and long streets like London'. Three decades later Daniel Defoe was to receive the same impression, adding that a former prisoner of the Duke of Marlborough, the Count Tallard, had laid out a beautiful parterre during his confinement, but added 'it does not gain by English keeping'. Defoe, too, refers to handsome town houses.

Between 1689 and 1761 there were 19 Parliaments elected. Approximately 2,000 freemen in Nottingham had the vote, but most of them were controlled by either the staunchly Whig Dukes of Newcastle or else by their political opponents the Tory Barons Middleton. As A. C. Wood has put it: 'It was government of the many by the few; but there is little to show that this was resented before the advent of the industrial revolution'.

Nottingham, however, had its advocates of parliamentary reform. One of these was John Cartwright, the younger brother of the more famous Anglican priest-cum-inventor Edmund Cartwright. In 1776 he issued a pamphlet urging that there should be annual elections, universal (male?) suffrage, the payment of Members and secret ballots – four of the demands of the Chartists half a century later. Four years later he formed a Constitutional Society in Nottingham and, although he won the support of the powerful Duke of Portland, he failed to win one of the two Nottingham seats. In 1785 he declared his support for William Pitt the Younger's own plans for parliamentary reform. In the 1802 general election there was riotous behaviour (including the singing of the 'Marseillaise'), which forced one of the sitting members, Daniel Coke, to withdraw his candidature. He appealed to the House of Commons to declare the subsequent election of the Radical Joseph Birch and the Tory Admiral Sir John Warren invalid on the grounds of intimidation – which the Commons agreed the following March. This enabled Coke to defeat Birch in the re-run contest. At the same time the Commons added a rider calling on the county's Justices of the Peace to take over the administration of law and order in Nottingham from that town's own bench. This measure remained in force until well after the battle of Waterloo.

By 1815 overcrowding in Nottingham had become so acute that a population that expanded five-fold in the previous 100 years was now packed tightly within the old walled medieval town. All told there were 8,000 back-to-back houses crammed into 132 streets, off which ran 308 courts and alleyways. Failure to enclose the open fields, and the

92

proximity of the hallowed estates of the two rival magnates (the Duke of Newcastle in his Castle mansion and Lord Middleton at Wollaton Hall), effectively ruled out the possibility of spilling out into suburbs until after the Nottingham Enclosure of 1845. As a result of this insanitary occupation of the town it has been estimated that the life expectancy of the poorest fell below 20 years!

Yet within the confines of Nottingham there were two Assembly Rooms in Low Pavement, Thurland Hall in Griddlesmith Gate (the former home of the Earls of Clare), a theatre in St Mary's Gate and the more salubrious residential areas that were illuminated by no less than 250 oil lamps by 1762 – the first gas lamps made their appearance in the town in 1819. Nottingham General Hospital opened its doors in 1781, and the local asylum in 1812, both supported by voluntary subscriptions.

Nottingham's council was largely in the hands of Whig nonconformists by the early part of the 19th century, including the Allen, Fellowes, Swann and Wakefield families. Indeed, four out of every five officers of the corporation, 20 of the councillors and aldermen, and the town clerk all worshipped at the same chapel. No balance sheets were ever published, nor did the corporation attempt to tackle the growing problem of local slums.

When the great debates on the Reform Bill began, seven out of the eight members who represented either the town or the rest of the county were in favour of this legislation. The news of its rejection reached Nottingham at the height of the annual Goose Fair. Bells were tolled and the premises of those against the Bill, such as bookseller William Bemrose, were attacked by mobs who believed naively that parliamentary reform was the panacea which would end unemployment and bad harvests. An attempt to break open the prison failed with the loss of three lives. On the following day, Sunday 8 October 1831, the Riot Act had to be read and the 15th Hussars were called from their barracks to help control the situation. On the Monday 20,000 people attended a Reform Rally in the Market Place. Although this appears to have passed off relatively peacefully, one mob from Sneinton sacked Colwick Hall and, thwarted in their plans to storm the prison again, they set fire to the empty shell of the Castle as a symbolic gesture, along with Lenton Hall and William Lowe's silk mill at Beeston: these latter properties were burnt on the night of 11 October. Only the presence of the Yeomanry kept the mob at bay when they tried to do the same to Wollaton Hall. The curfew was imposed nightly at 5.00 p.m., and in January 1832 a special commission tried eight of the rioters, sentencing three of them to death. The Duke of Newcastle was awarded £21,000 as compensation for the loss of his semi-derelict mansion on Castle Rock!

Severns building, now the Nottingham Lace Centre

In the 19th century Nottingham was very much a growing industrial town. There were three principal breweries in 1800, which were located in Goose Gate (Thomas Simpson), Leen Bridge (Messrs. Teverill & Co.) and Poplar Place (Henry Green & Co.).

In the lace industry bobbin-net manufacture was established not only in Nottingham itself, but also in the outlying suburbs of Arnold, Basford, Beeston, Lenton and Radford. Little girls were employed as threaders. However, machines were already being smuggled illegally to France, especially in the 1830s, whilst some of the lace workers themselves emigrated to that country where wages were reported to be 60 per cent higher. Yet towards the end of the 19th century Nottingham's lace industry had a renaissance; the number of machines operating increased sharply from 1,050 in 1873 (in 224 factories) to 2,250 ten years later. By 1890 there were over 500 lace factories in the town, employing a combined workforce of over 17,000 operatives.

Yet just as the lace industry began to revive, so the hosiery industry declined. Marc Brunel's tricoteur machine, which enabled stockings to be knitted as one piece, did not reach Nottingham until 1845 – some thirty years after its invention. By the mid-century there were 10,500 knitting frames in the town, the vast bulk of their products being exported.

The Trent Bridge with its 10 arches had been rebuilt after the Civil War. In 1871 it was replaced by the present structure, which was both more elegant and more practical, allowing larger vessels to pass upstream. The Humber keels were amongst these, 61 ft. 6 in. long and with a beam of 15 ft. 8 in. When the days of sail gave way in the early 20th century to those of petrol and diesel engines, some of these keels were demasted and converted into ordinary barges to be towed behind tugs. In 1926 the river itself was greatly improved at Gunthorpe, Hazleford, Holme and Stoke Bardolph. Three years later the Gunthorpe Bridge (which had been erected in 1873) was replaced by a new structure. Then in 1955 a brand new site was chosen for a road crossing of the Trent at Clifton, effectively making redundant the nearby Wilford toll bridge of 1870.

Over the past century Nottingham industry has been dominated by three firms each of which has become not only nationally but internationally famous in its field of enterprise. Each of the three was founded by a far-sighted man.

Victorian ironwork on the Trent Bridge

Born in 1839, the son of a Baptist solicitor, John Player moved from Saffron Walden in 1862 to become a drapery assistant in Nottingham. Within a comparatively short period he had left his employer to establish his own shop on Beastmarket Hill, dealing in agricultural manures and

MANUFACTURERS OF
Lace Window Nets, Blinds, Valances & Curtains

Also

Head - rests,

Chesterfield Covers,

Anti- macassars,

Bed-spreads,

Squares and Runners

Specialists in

Artificial Silk and Cotton Novelties of every description made on a Lace Curtain Machine

Telegraphic Addresses:
Carey, Nottingham
Garrison, Gent.,
          London

CAREY & SONS, LTD.,
Salerooms:--45, Broad Street, NOTTINGHAM   21a, Old Change, LONDON
FACTORY   SOUTHWELL, Notts

Telephones :
Nottingham 41011-2
London : City 8174
Southwell 47

Advertisement for Nottingham lace from The Empire Mail, *June 1928.*

Player's sailor trade mark

seeds. To supplement his income, John Player bought loose tobacco, which he resold as cheap 'screws' to working men. Gradually it was this subsidiary side of his business which became so financially successful that in 1877 he purchased a small tobacco factory situated in Broad Marsh. This had been opened in 1823 by William Wright and employed 150 workers. Player decided to put cigarettes into paper packets, each of which bore his new registered trade mark of Nottingham Castle. Later, in 1883, he changed this to a sailor, adding the famous lifebuoy in 1888. Three years later H.M.S. *Britannia* and *Hero* were added. The *final* design was, however, based on a painting by A. D. McCormick and introduced in 1927.

In the early 1880s John Player bought a 30-acre site at Radford on which he planned to erect a new factory, since his sales now extended well outside the Nottingham area. Known as the Castle Factory (due to the trade mark of the time), it opened in April 1884, just prior to Player's premature death. This new works had one of the largest rooms built by that time, 300 feet long by 60 feet wide. A 300 h.p. engine was installed to drive the machinery.

John's sons were only children when he died, and it was not until 1893 that John Dane Player and William Goodacre Player were old enough to take over the firm. By 1898 two more factories were built on the Radford site, bringing the total workforce to one thousand. A fifth of them were girls, nicknamed 'Player's Angels'. They each made up to 2,000 cigarettes per *day* by hand. However there were also five Elliott machines, each of which was capable of producing 200 cigarettes per *minute*.

Faced with the undercutting price tactics of the American tobacco monopolist, James Buchanan 'Buck' Duke, in 1901 John Player & Sons joined with 12 other British manufacturers to form the Imperial Tobacco Company to ward off this unwanted cut-throat competition. John Player's sons remained on Imperial's Board until their retirement in 1926. By 1914, 2,500 workers were employed on the expanding Radford site. During the First World War, as in the Boer War, Players issued cigarette cards with patriotic themes such as 'Regimental Uniforms' and 'War Trophies'. In the post-war era smoking was popularised by such eminent people as H.R.H. the Prince of Wales (who visited the factories in 1923) and the novelist Sapper with his detective hero Bulldog Drummond. Women in large numbers began to smoke cigarettes too. So by 1928 the Players workforce had reached 5,000, adding a further 50 per cent to this total within the next five years as a result of the building of yet two more factories at Radford. In 1972 the £14,000,000 Horizon factory was built on a new 45-acre site at Lenton.

Early Boot's delivery van

34. Sir Richard Arkwright (1732-92) who helped to establish Nottingham's textile industry.

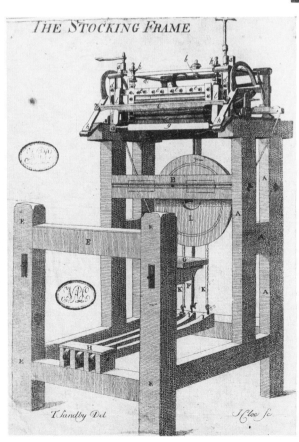

THE STOCKING FRAME

T. Sandby Del   J. Cloe sc

35. A 1751 engraving of a stocking frame, one of the most important inventions in the county's textile history.

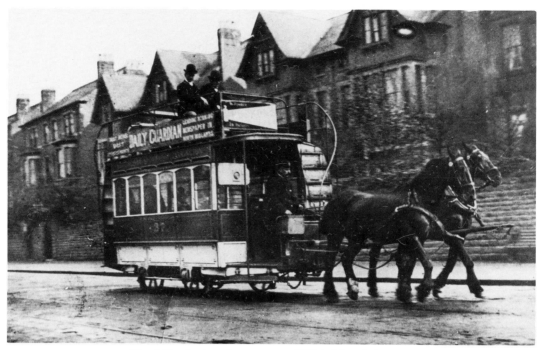

36. A Nottingham horse tram *c.*1900 in Mansfield Road.

37. Newark coach station, 1933, with a fleet of Lincolnshire Road car vehicles awaiting departure.

38. Mansfield railway viaduct straddles the town's centre and is still in use for coal traffic.

39. Newark railway station, built in the Early Italianate style for the Midland in 1836.

40. Tom Barton, the motor bus pioneer, demonstrates with a lighted taper that an early diesel engine will not explode, 1930.

41. Wilford Suspension Bridge over the Trent at Nottingham is now restricted to cyclists and pedestrians and freed from tolls.

Jesse Boot was born in 1850, the son of a local farm labourer, whose sideline was making and selling herbal remedies. When Jesse was 13 he left school to help his widowed mother Mary run her small herbal shop in Goose Gate. Studying in his few spare hours to better his poor education, Jesse Boot took over his mother's business in 1877. At once he placed an advertisement in the *Nottingham Daily Express* which listed 128 items he sold, including hair restorers, charcoal biscuits, cooling powders and the already famous Beecham's Pills. In 1884 he employed a bellringer to tour the town's streets announcing his bargain prices for soap. All these ploys brought him such increased custom that he was able to move into more spacious premises, which included a workshop, where from 1885 he began to make his own preparations. During the final two decades of the 19th century Boot started to open branches not only in Nottingham itself, but also in surrounding towns. Each new opening had its razmataz, for Jesse was always a showman at heart. In addition he became involved in the mail order business.

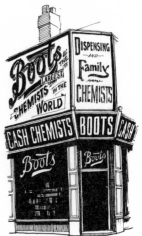

Boot's first shop, Nottingham

When he married Florence Rowe, daughter of a Jersey stationer, in 1886, she persuaded him to expand his business to include books, notepaper and cosmetics. She also took a motherly interest in the growing workforce of young girls from impoverished homes. Boot's first factory of 1892 was supplemented by many more, including a soap works in 1928. Just before his death in 1931 a new 300-acre site was acquired, and in due course premises were built there to include research facilities into pharmaceuticals and agricultural chemicals. On the retail side Boot's eventually increased their range of different items to 50,000. In 1920 Jesse Boot had sold his controlling interest in his company to the United Drug Company of the United States. However, when, in 1933, that conglomerate fell on hard times during the recession his son, John Campbell Boot, led a consortium of British financiers to re-purchase the company. Jesse himself was knighted, mainly for his philanthropy, in 1903. He was created a baronet in 1917 and raised to the peerage as 1st Baron Trent two years before his death.

An early entrepreneur in the sphere of building bicycles was Tom Humber, who based himself at Beeston. He built to his own design the orthodox style tricycle with chain transmission, direct steering and pedals. By 1883 he had reduced the weight of his racing machines from an average of 110 lbs. to 50 lbs.

It was in 1886 that R. M. Woodhead, a clever mechanic, with a French engineer by the name of Paul Angois, and one Ellis, a financier, formed a partnership to build bicycles and tricycles in a small factory in Russell Street. The bicycles were of the 'ordinary' (or so-called 'Penny-farthing') variety, invented by James Starley of Coventry in 1870. The Nottingham

Boot's centenary logo

Raleigh bicycle, 1888

firm also began to assemble the newer 'Safety' cycle, which had been designed by H. J. Lawson as early as 1879 under his trade mark of 'Bicyclette'. The new business chose the trade name 'Raleigh' for their products, since this was the name of a nearby street. As bicycling became more popular, the infant firm expanded and additional workshop space was rented.

In December 1888 a businessman called Frank Bowden, having ridden a Raleigh tricycle whilst undergoing a health cure at Arachan in south-west France, out of curiosity visited the works on his return to England. He was so impressed by what he saw that he bought out the partners, subsequently launching his own Raleigh Cycle Company Ltd. The first Raleigh machines had 'spoon' brakes acting on the rear tyres and anti-vibration springs at the fork crowns. Raleigh was amongst the first manufacturers to take out a licence to fit Dunlop tyres, when these first appeared in 1889. Three years later Raleigh entered the racing field as a rival to Humber. Bowden persuaded the great American amateur racing cyclist Zimmerman to use a Raleigh in his bid to win the English National Championships. Zimmerman was successful in three out of four races. In 1896 G. P. Mills transferred from Humbers to take up the post of works manager, and he introduced the cross-framed cycles and tandems to the Lenton factory. Edward Glover (another engineer with Raleigh at this time) invented a method to make cycle parts from pressed steel instead of from the much heavier castings and forgings. This enabled tubular fork crowns to be fitted.

In this century Raleigh has become one of the leading manufacturers of racing cycles in the world, and in 1980 its team won a record 12 stages in the Tour de France. Parallel to these developments has been the introduction in 1965 of the RSW model with its 16 in. wheels, which also came in a folding version suitable for stowing in car boots. Later still with the growth in the popularity amongst youngsters of BMX riding came the 'Chopper' in 1969. This sold 750,000 machines in the model's initial 10 years. It was followed by the equally successful 'Grifter' in 1976 with its crash-pad handlebars. A third model, the 'Burner' launched in 1982, has had an even more immediate success in this new field.

Nottingham grew from a town of 28,801 inhabitants at the time of the first national Census in 1801 to 239,743 a century later – an increase in population of 732 per cent: a rate only exceeded in the county's towns by the relative newcomers Hucknall (919 per cent) and Kirkby-in-Ashfield (937 per cent). In contrast long-established towns like Mansfield and Newark only recorded 258 per cent and 123 per cent respectively over the same period.

The growth of Nottingham and its suburbs necessitated a widely spread and increasingly intensive public transport system. That which developed within the city itself will be examined in chapter XVI; this chapter will deal with the systems which fed into Nottingham from outside its limits. The fast expanding town of West Bridgford had its own distinctive brown and cream buses run by the Urban District Council which had begun a service using Dennis double-deckers back in 1914. However, until 1927 they were not permitted to bring their own vehicles over Trent Bridge and into the city centre. Eventually, in 1968, this slightly eccentric fleet (whose new vehicles were allocated numbers on the basis that there must always be the same quantity of odd and even numbers, and where huge route numbers were carried for those with poor eyesight on a foggy day!) was taken over by Nottingham City Transport.

At the time of the September 1908 Goose Fair in Nottingham Market Place, Tom Barton ran a Durham Churchill char-a-banc to transport people from his native Long Eaton into the city. This was such a success that he built a network of routes in the Nottingham area, which was extended in the First World War by a contract to carry workers from Nottingham to the Chilwell Shell Filling Factory. Tom Barton also pioneered the diesel engined bus. Bartons, with the Robin Hood badge on their red, maroon and cream coaches, are still a familiar sight in the streets of Nottingham, as are also the luxury vehicles of Skill's Motor Coaches Ltd., started by Mr. A. Skill soon after the First World War, using a converted lorry as a bus. During the Second World War he acquired a stage carriage route between Nottingham and East Bridgford. Principally the firm has concentrated on long distance coach routes and excursions for Nottingham clientele, although under deregulation in October 1986 it has ventured into Lincolnshire to take over the Sunday service between Lincoln and Skegness.

Another transport entrepreneur was Mr. C. T. Dabell of Gotham, who began to operate a small Guy single-decker bus into Nottingham in March 1926. On 19 January 1928 he formed the South Notts. Bus Company Ltd., which continues to work this route. As from 1951 vehicles have been diverted to serve the Clifton estate – one of the largest housing complexes in Europe.

In the 19th century the growing city aspired to an institution of higher learning. Further education in its most embryonic and basic form had begun in Nottingham as early as 1798, when the Methodist William Singleton joined forces with the Quaker Samuel Fox to open the first adult school in England. Here both men and women were taught to read the Bible, to write and to perform simple computations. By 1815

Replica of Tom Barton's original charabanc

Jesse Boot, 1st Lord Trent

some of the local Sunday Schools were also providing instruction for adults. Then in 1824 the concept of establishing a Mechanics' Institute (alias an Artisans' Library) was mooted, but it was not until 1837 that this plan came to fruition with the help of some wealthy backers led by banker John Smith Wright. Initially it was able to boast of a membership of 600, and a library containing over 700 volumes. At first in rented accommodation in St James's Street, it moved into its own premises in 1845. As from 1856 it received financial assistance from the Department of Science and Art. The institution survived a serious fire in 1867 and became the focal point for university extension courses, planned by James Stuart, which started in April 1871.

The original syllabus for such courses included subjects like Political Economy, the Science of Health, the Constitutional History of England, and English Literature. This was aided by Cambridge University, which appointed a syndicate of local tutors for the autumn term of 1873. The foundation stone for the new college in Shakespeare Street was laid on 27 September four years later, with Her Majesty's Leader of the Opposition, W. E. Gladstone, as one of the speakers on that occasion. The doors of the new building were opened in 1881.

It was at this stage affiliated to Cambridge, but by the turn of the century some students were sitting for London external degrees, thus forging links with that university that were to result in the institution becoming the University College, Nottingham, under a charter of incorporation of August 1903. In the early years of this century plans for an East Midlands University were discussed, but these were scuppered when Leicester withdrew from the scheme in June 1923.

Sir Jesse Boot (once described as 'the humble herbalist from Hockley') presented the College with the 35-acre 'Highfield' site, which was renamed University Park. Originally he had acquired the property to build his own equivalent to Port Sunlight or Bourneville. In 1922, as a result of Boot's donation of £50,000, work began on the first buildings, which were officially opened by Their Majesties George V and Queen Mary on 10 July 1928. The site was extended by a further 20 acres in 1932. Full university status was granted by royal charter on 20 August 1948. The Queen's Medical Centre was added some twenty years later, whilst in the early 1980s the 14-acre Highfields Science Park was opened on the other side of University Boulevard to encourage industry to engage in high technology and innovation, working closely with the University's own research teams.

After the passing of the First Reform Act in 1832 Nottingham usually returned two Liberal M.P.s, including the famous baronet Sir John Hobhouse. But in the general election of 1847 Hobhouse was defeated when a strange combination of Conservative John Walter jnr. and the Chartist leader Fergus O'Connor was elected. On certain occasions before the passing of the Secret Ballot Act of 1872 petitions were submitted by defeated candidates to declare the election null and void. Sometimes, as in a by-election in August 1842 and the general election of July 1865, they were successful. At other times (in 1841, 1843 and 1869) such petitions were dismissed. Under the terms of the Third Reform Act of 1884 Nottingham itself was divided into three single-member constituencies. Nottingham West was a Liberal stronghold, whilst (apart from the 1885 and 1906 general elections) Nottingham South returned Conservative members. Nottingham East was more a political barometer, returning Liberals in 1885, 1886 (both elections), 1892 and 1906, but Conservatives in 1895, 1900 and 1910 (both elections). As from 1918 the city was redivided into four constituencies, of which initially only Nottingham West was held by Labour. That party captured Nottingham South in 1929, but was not to take Nottingham Central and Nottingham East until the Attlee landslide of July 1945. Although the Tories regained Nottingham South in 1955, the other three seats have usually remained in Labour hands. In 1974 representation of Nottingham was cut to three M.P.s: the East, North and West seats all being won by Labour candidates. However the overwhelming victory of the Conservatives in June 1983 resulted in the Tories holding all the city's seats for the first time since 1874!

Nottingham has catered for the sporting tastes of its people for a long time. Defoe mentions the horse races held on the outskirts of Nottingham, which he must have witnessed personally for he describes them as 'a most glorious show', with 'an assembly of gentlemen of quality, that not Banstead Down [i.e. Epsom] and New Market Heath produces better company, better horses, or shows the horse and master's skill better'.

Trent Bridge became one of the earliest centres of cricket in the East Midlands. In the 1830s the landlord of the *Bell Inn*, William Clarke, encouraged this game. It is often difficult to differentiate between teams which represented just the town and just the county. Certainly the first recorded away county match was at Brighton, against Sussex, in August 1835. The Nottinghamshire County Cricket Club as such was founded at Trent Bridge in spring 1841, but was reorganised on 11 December 1866. Under the captaincy of George Parr (1856-70) the side improved so much that they became County Champions in 1875, 1879, 1880, 1883, 1884, 1885 and 1886, as well as sharing the title in 1873, 1882 and 1889. In this century they have not only provided one of the four established provincial test match venues, but many world-class players such as Harold Larwood (played 1924-38), Bill Voce (1927-52), Joe Hardstaff

Nottingham University

101

jnr. (1930-55) and Reg Simpson (1946-63). They have only won the County Championship on three occasions (1907, 1929 and 1981), in spite of having in their side two of the greatest all-rounders of this century. Gary Sobers (1968-74) not only scored 7,041 runs for the team, but also had a haul of 281 wickets, whilst since 1978 the team has included New Zealander Richard Hadlee. George Gunn (1902-32) was their most prolific batsman: in a county record of 583 appearances he scored 31,592 runs.

Within sight of the Trent Bridge cricket ground is that of Nottingham Forest Football Club, founded in 1865, although not elected to the Football League until 1892, when they joined the newly-formed Division One. After the 1905/6 season they were relegated to Division Two, but the ensuing season became that division's champions and returned to the top. In 1909 they created a Division One record when they thrashed Leicester Fosse 12 – 0. Although twice winners of the F.A. Cup (beating Derby County in 1898 and Luton Town in 1959), they have only been Division One Champions once – in 1977/8. Abroad they won two successive European Cups, beating Malmo in 1979 and S.V. Hamburg in 1980.

Neighbouring Notts. County Football Club on the other side of the river have the proud claim that they are the oldest club still in the Football League, having been founded in 1862. Since the League was formed in 1888 they have played a record of over three thousand five hundred league fixtures. They may have beaten Thornhill United 15 – 0 in the first round of the F.A. Cup on 24 October 1885, but in the League they have not excelled like Forest. Much of their time has been spent outside Division One, although during the 1890/1 season they did finish third in the premier division. There was a strange case in the 1909/ 10 season when Notts. County sold their rights in the first round of the Cup to Bradford City, who went on to win that fixture 4 – 2. The sum that changed hands was £1,000. Inter-club rivalry between the two Nottingham sides existed from the earliest days, and in 1889 County were fine £5 by the League for 'poaching' player Tinsley Lindley from Forest.

Nottingham has also produced the ice-dancing champion pair of Christopher Dean and Jayne Torvill, who won the gold medal at the 1984 Winter Olympics held at Sarajevo. They also went on to become European and World Champions.

XV   Nineteenth-Century Nottinghamshire

The beginning of the 19th century brings our first reliable population statistics. The Census of 1801 showed that, of the 140,350 who lived in Nottinghamshire at that date, only 40 per cent were living in what could be described as towns. Indeed only six urban areas had over 2,000 inhabitants, including Nottingham itself, the population of which was recorded as 28,801. This made it four times larger than the county's second town, Newark, which had a population of 6,730 in 1801. Mansfield came third with 5,988 residents. In its turn it was almost double the size of fourth-placed Worksop which had 3,263 residents. The fifth and sixth towns in this population league were respectively Sutton-in-Ashfield (2,801) and Southwell (2,305). In addition there were five smaller towns of over 1,000 people: East Retford (1,948), Hucknall Torkard (1,497), Mansfield Woodhouse (1,112), Bingham (1,082) and Kirkby-in-Ashfield (1,002).

Crimean War canon, Retford

By the 1851 Census the county's population had almost doubled to 270,427, and by this mid-century date 48.5 per cent of Nottinghamshire's inhabitants were living in communities of over 1,000 souls. Three towns that now exceeded this figure were Hucknall Huthwaite (1,150), Tuxford (1,211) and Warsop (1,398). The first eight towns had retained their rank order of size, but below that level Kirkby-in-Ashfield and Mansfield Woodhouse had exchanged their 9th and 11th positions as coal mining continued to expand apace.

At the close of this century the population of the county had reached 514,628, now with 70 per cent residing in urban areas. Mansfield (21,441) had ousted Newark (14,992) from second position. Nottingham itself was by this time no less than 11 times larger in population than any other town in the county. Worksop (16,112) had moved up into third place, followed by Hucknall Torkard (15,250), Newark and Sutton-in-Ashfield (14,866). As far as percentage increase is concerned Hucknall Torkard (413 per cent) had expanded faster than any other Nottinghamshire town during the second half of this century, followed by Kirkby-in-Ashfield (340 per cent). Again the boom in coal mining must take much of the credit for these swift increases on the western fringe of

Cast iron parish boundary mark near Nottingham Castle

Donkey engine, Beckingham

the county. The only 'new' town to emerge during the period 1851 to 1901 was West Bridgford. The advent of a public transport system between Trent Bridge and the centre of Nottingham enabled West Bridgford to become a dormitory town for workers in the city. Thus its population had mushroomed from a paltry 258 in 1851 to 7,018 by 1901.

As has been indicated above, the coal mining industry made great strides throughout the 19th century. Working pits in 1801 included Beauvale Abbey, Beggarlee, Bilborough, Bramcote, Brinsley New (alias Fenton), Brinsley Old, Cossall, Dunshill, Eastwood, Greasley, Hucknall (or Blackwell), Limes (near Greasley), Shile (north-west of Hucknall), Skegby, Trowell Moor and Wollaton. Some of these pits were now relatively deep. For example, that at Nuthall was sunk to 480 feet. The coal was transported by barges on the Erewash and Nottingham Canals, but in 1819 a mineral tramway was laid down between Pinxton Wharf and Mansfield, with iron wagons pulled by horses; inertia was employed after Kirkby Summit had been reached. This tramway was in use until the Erewash Valley railway line was opened in 1847.

The centre of the coal mining industry shifted to Cinder Hill, Basford, in 1841 when the Duke of Newcastle had shafts sunk to a depth of 666 feet. Thirteen years later that magnate opened other mines at Shire Oaks where there were deep seams of furnace coal, Hazel's coal and top hard coal – the latter being reached at 1,527 feet below the surface. This was the first successful attempt to penetrate the Permian stratum that lay above the coal measures at this point. By 1860 there were 21 collieries in Nottinghamshire: a total that gradually increased to 31 by 1907, when there were 16 separate companies locally involved in this industry.

These mines led to ribbon development along the Erewash valley, including the growth of Eastwood, where David Herbert Lawrence was born in a typical miner's terrace house on 11 September 1885.

There were dramatic increases in the amount of coal produced in the Nottinghamshire field in the second half of the 19th century. Rising from an output of 732,666 tons in 1862, it reached 6,970,224 tons by 1897, and went on to 11,728,886 tons a decade later. Likewise, the number of men employed in this industry within the county advanced from 23,024 in 1897 to 35,415 by 1907.

Apart from in the centre of Nottingham, the textile industry was still flourishing on the western side of the county. For example, in 1839 2,272 workers were employed in 21 different mills. Of this total of manufactories the largest number (13) were involved in the cotton trade, located at Bulwell, Cuckney, Lowdham, Mansfield and Sutton-in-Ashfield. Four of the other mills were engaged in the production of worsted cloth in Radford and Sutton Bonington. The final quartet were silk mills in Nottingham and Southwell.

42. Lord Byron (1788-1824) who lived at
Newstead Abbey.

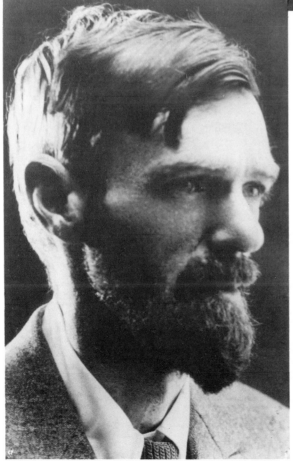

43. D.H.Lawrence (1885-1930), the novelist, who was
born and grew up in Eastwood.

44. The mausoleum of the 4th Duke of Newcastle, built at Milton after the death of his wife in 1822.

45. The Georgian *Newcastle Arms* beside the old Great North Road at Tuxford.

46. The prosperity which some Methodists at least had won by 1882 is reflected in the grand Gothic lines of East Retford Wesleyan chapel.

47. St John's church, Colston Bassett, built in 1892 by the local squire as a monument to his dead son and wife.

48. (*above*) Clifton Colliery, 1895, with miners boarding the pit cage for their ascent at the end of a shift.

49. (*left*) Modern gypsum mining, an industry that has its roots in medieval times.

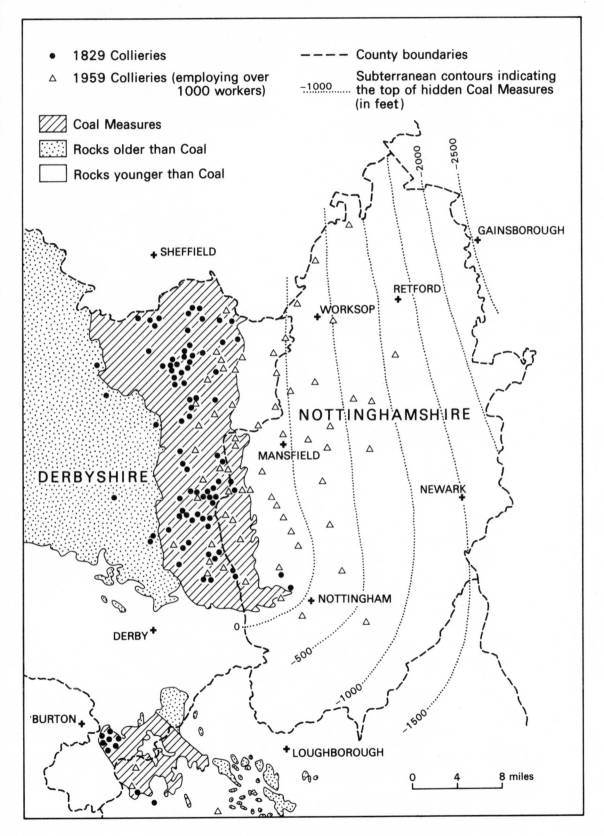

Legend

- ● 1829 Collieries
- △ 1959 Collieries (employing over 1000 workers)

- – – – County boundaries
- ·····-1000···· Subterranean contours indicating the top of hidden Coal Measures (in feet)

- ▨ Coal Measures
- ⠿ Rocks older than Coal
- ☐ Rocks younger than Coal

Map labels

-2000
-2500

GAINSBOROUGH

+ SHEFFIELD

RETFORD

WORKSOP

NOTTINGHAMSHIRE

MANSFIELD

DERBYSHIRE

NEWARK

0

-500

+ NOTTINGHAM

+ DERBY

-1000

-1500

BURTON +

+ LOUGHBOROUGH

0   4   8 miles

Map 12. Nottinghamshire Coal Industry.

Taking one particular case history, Humphrey Hollins was a brazier who had moved from Ashby-de-la-Zouch in Leicestershire into Nottingham soon after 1700. Here he continued his craft successfully, for by 1739 his grandson, Humphrey Hollins III, had risen to be Sheriff, and eventually became Mayor in 1762 and again in 1769. It was the latter's son Henry Hollins who founded the textile manufacturing company, which has been based in the Mansfield-Nottingham area for the past two centuries and is internationally famous.

At his original Mansfield factory he employed many Poor Law apprentices from as far away as Birmingham, Braintree, Doncaster, Hereford and Lambeth to run his mills. J. Throsby, writing in 1790, remarked about them, 'There are children from the Foundling Hospital, London, who are employed at the mills and are kept in excellent order. They live in cottages, built for the purpose, under the care of superintendants . . . an apothecary attends them at stated times to preserve health. They are trained to the duties of religion and are fed plentifully.'

After 1821 Australian Merino wool was blended with cotton by Hollins so that both could be spun together into a single mixed yarn on machinery for cotton. In 1844 the Cuckney Mill was closed and 11 years later William Hollins & Company rented the Sherwood Mills, off Nottingham Road, Mansfield, on a temporary basis, before moving their business into Nottingham. Here Richard Tucker's starch factory was acquired for Lenton Mill, and was converted into a textile manufactory. However, in 1862 a further move was made to the Old Silk Mill in Radford. The existing facilities on this site were added to in 1864 when a new Merino mill and a dye and bleach works were opened. And it was here in 1891, after many experimental yarns had been tried, that Viyella cloth was first produced. The early production went for men's striped shirts and nightshirts. The trade name Viyella was derived from the place name Via Gellia (near Matlock) where Hollins had another mill. But the locals referred to the site as 'Vi Jella', hence its adoption by the company, together with their famous 'Day & Night Wear' trademark (1896) immortalised by a poem written by one of their travellers, William Firley:

> For Hunting, for Shooting, a luxury real,
> For Cycling and Tennis, the long sought ideal,
> For Bathing and Fishing, for Sea side & Boating,
> For Tailor-made Dresses & Smart Winter Coating,
> For Layettes & Lingerie, Gowns, Frocks & Trousseau,
> Once buy it, and try it, for ever you'll do so,
> From torture to comfort it leads so we think,
> Our 'Viyella's' unrivalled because it Don't Shrink!

Brewing continued to be an important industry in 19th-century Nottinghamshire towns, and Newark was regarded as the centre of the whole industry in England. This was in spite of the growth of the temperance movement with its provision of coffee taverns for working men. In 1882, Viscountess Ossington built an impressive coffee tavern on the banks of the Trent, almost within a stone's throw of many Newark breweries. At that date D. H. Lawrence's mother Lydia was remonstrating with her drunken husband on the other side of the county. East Retford was no longer one of the more important brewing centres, but Worksop had taken its place with maltings such as the Clinton kilns, run by J. M. Threlfall in 1852. Outside Newark, at Carlton-on-Trent, Hole's maltings were doing good business. In 1823/4 Nottinghamshire produced 24,309 barrels of strong beer and 5,472 barrels of table beers, which together had required 100,452 bushels of malt. By this time, barley malt had replaced hops as one of the main ingredients of locally-brewed beer. As late as 1800, however, approximately 1,100 acres of hops were grown, chiefly around Retford, Southwell and Tuxford.

When Arthur Young toured Nottinghamshire during the years 1768-1770 he noted three principal crops used in arable rotation: turnips; barley or oats; rye. However much of the county had a four-crop rotation of turnips, barley, clover or peas, and wheat. He saw an increased acreage under potatoes and carrots – the latter being particularly conspicuous north of Newark and at Arnold on the outskirts of Nottingham. Here farmer Cope sold his crop in Mansfield to feed its growing urban population. At the northern end of the county Young saw hops growing at Ordsall, next to Retford. Later, in 1794, Robert Lowe reported in his *A General View of the Agriculture of the County of Nottingham* that 'Many of the principal farmers carry on agriculture with great spirit, adopting the best practices of other counties'. He added that there had been many improvements during the previous quarter of a century.

Before 1700 only 12 per cent of Nottinghamshire had been enclosed. However in the 18th century 158 Enclosure Acts were passed, covering over half the county, leaving approximately 35 per cent still to be enclosed after 1800, through a further 79 Acts. One of the greatest factors in this movement was the attitude of the largest landowners, and especially the dukes, which is perhaps why most of the 18th-century enclosures took place on the Keuper Marl and the northern portion of the Bunter sandstone in the heart of the Dukeries. The earliest enclosures, on the other hand, had taken place in the Nottingham area, though not in Nottingham itself, as was seen in the previous chapter. Significantly, the final enclosures were around Laxton, which became famous for retaining its open fields until the present day (1987).

Amongst the minority crops was flax, which was grown on the lower reaches of the Trent, where warping took place (i.e. special sluices were used to irrigate the land along the river bank). There were flax mills near Gainsborough. However, by 1880 less than ten acres of this crop were cultivated in the county. Also connected with the textile industry was meld (or dyer's week), which produced a yellow dye. This was grown, with barley and clover, in the north-western corner of the county at Ranskill and Scrooby. The cultivation of liquorice around Worksop ended before 1790, although it continued around Mansfield Woodhouse.

Another 'crop found near Newark (at Barnby-le-Willows), near Retford and opposite Gainsborough at Beckingham, Bole and Cottam, as well as around Kegworth in the Soar valley was osiers. Four varieties were cultivated. The cricket-bat willow lived up to its name, whilst the crack willow, white willow and willow shrub all went to the basket weaving trade.

Turning to livestock farming, in the 18th century the principal breed of cattle had been the Longhorn. The Shorthorn only made its appearance on the local scene towards 1800. In 1852 Amos Cruickshank of Aberdeenshire visited John Wilkinson of Lenton to purchase some of his Shorthorn bulls, amongst which was the famous champion Lancaster Cornet. During the Agricultural Depression in the final quarter of the 19th century the number of cattle raised in the county fell only slightly from 79,326 head in 1875 to 77,276 in 1881. Irish beasts were brought in to be fattened before proceeding to slaughterhouses in the south.

There had been an indigenous Forest breed of sheep, but some farmers crossed them with Lincolnshire Longwools and New Leicesters by the late 1840s. The county's sheep farmers had benefited in the 18th century from Robert Bakewell's famous flocks at Disley, just over the Derbyshire border. Whereas in 1800 the average flock in Nottinghamshire was between 50 and 100 animals, by 1850 many flocks had over 500 sheep in them. Soon afterwards, however, much pasture land was ploughed up during the Crimean War. In the first years of the Agricultural Depression sheep farming seems to have suffered more than cattle raising, for there was a drop in the county's total from 284,945 animals in 1875 to 216,563 six years later, presumably caused by the importation of massive quantities of Australian wool by the fast clippers.

Pigs were very much a minority form of animal husbandry during the last century, their numbers falling from 26,739 to 23,435 between 1875 and 1881. However, many labourers continued to keep a pig for their family's sustenance.

In his book, Robert Lowe mentioned that most farms, their outbuildings and labourers' cottages were built either of brick and tile (on the

Keuper Marls) or else of stone (on the western fringes of the county). There had been massive rebuilding in the 18th century, a process which continued as late as the 1880s. The farmhouses often had gypsum upper floors as a fire precaution. The farm buildings themselves continued to be located in the main village streets instead of being resited, out of the nucleus, in the newly-enclosed fields. The exceptions were mainly in the northernmost parts of the county around Misterton and Scrooby.

As a result of the 1832 Reform Act the county's representation was doubled and at the same time it was divided into two twin-member constituencies. In the southern Nottinghamshire seat two Liberals were elected, but as from the 1835 general election there was to one Liberal and one Conservative chosen, normally unopposed (apart from the 1852 general election, which ended ironically with one of each major party elected!), suggesting some form of consensus amongst the leading people in this half of the county. Oddly enough the only occasion when two Liberals were returned was in 1880 – the final general election before a further redistribution of seats under the terms of the Third Reform Act. However northern Nottinghamshire followed this practice only in 1835, 1852 and 1868, two Conservatives being returned in the elections of 1837, 1841, 1847 and 1874, whilst two Liberals were successful at the poll in 1857, 1859 and 1865. This may well have been due to the political influence of the powerful magnates in The Dukeries.

The virtually rotten borough of Newark remained a two-member seat until the passing of the 1884 Reform Act. Between 1832 and 1847 one of these members was a young Tory by the name of William Ewart Gladstone, who was later to switch his allegiance and became one of the most famous Liberal leaders and Prime Ministers. It was whilst he fought Newark that he became embroiled in a scandal over his electioneering expenses. From 1857 until 1880 the town was represented by two Liberals.

In 1884 the four county seats became separate single-member constituencies; at the same time Newark lost one of its members. Bassetlaw was a Conservative stronghold where the member was returned unopposed in 1886 and 1900, although the Liberals managed to capture the seat in their landslide victory in the 1906 general election. The other safe Conservative seat was that of Newark, where rarely did the Tory candidate have to face an ordeal through the ballot box – even in 1906! On the other hand both Mansfield and Rushcliffe remained staunchly Liberal until the First World War.

In Local Government there was much corruption at the beginning of the 19th century, and before the implementation of the Municipal Corporations Act of 1835. For example, the council at East Retford were

Nottingham City Hall

109

Colton Bassett church

Headstones from Southwell Minster

described by the Municipal Commissioners in 1833 as 'Self-chosen from a clan not only inferior in station and intelligence, but also branded with infamy or long continued and notorious bribery . . .'. From his country seat at Clumber Park the Duke of Newcastle exerted his influence over the town and its affairs, controlling shopkeepers who made up the council. This magnate's power was felt just as strongly in Newark where he was a principal landowner. Here he presided over the aldermen as they chose not only the Mayor, but also their own replacements.

On 30 March 1851 the unique Religious Census was taken throughout the country. Dr. John Gay has analysed its results county-by-county with some interesting conclusions. As far as Nottinghamshire is concerned the average level of church/chapel attendance at that date was between 60 and 70 per cent, placing it in the same percentile band as Lincolnshire and the East and North Ridings of Yorkshire, but above Derbyshire and the West Riding. Of the neighbouring counties, only Leicestershire had a higher attendance rate. This is reflected, too, when Nottingham itself is compared with other East Midland county towns. Again Nottinghamshire was similar to Lincolnshire in that between a quarter and one third attended Church of England services on census day. In comparison, between 30 and 40 per cent went instead to nonconformist places of worship. Of the various denominations which made up the latter grouping, Methodists (although they formed a smaller percentage than in neighbouring counties) still made up the largest body, although it must be remembered that at that date they had fragmented into Wesleyan, Primitive and New Connexion Methodists. The next group in size were the Baptists (mainly General rather than Particular), followed by Congregationalists and Presbyterians. Roman Catholics amounted to less than two per cent: only Lincolnshire of other East Midlands counties had a smaller proportion of worshippers.

In 1884 the huge diocese of York was divided, with Nottinghamshire being separated off to form the see of Southwell, where the ancient minster was raised to cathedral status. Here in 1984, to mark its centenary, the Queen distributed the Royal Maundy. In 1928 Derbyshire was removed from the diocese of Southwell and given its own see based on Derby. After the passing of the Catholic Emancipation Act in 1829 England was divided into districts, each administered by a Vicar-Apostolic appointed by the Holy See. In reality he fulfilled the functions of a bishop until the Roman Catholic hierarchy was restored in 1850. The following year Joseph Hendren, who had been the Vicar-Apostolic of the Western District, became the first Bishop of Nottingham. His diocese also included Derbyshire (until 1980), Leicestershire and Lincolnshire.

XVI   Twentieth-Century Nottinghamshire

The population of the county increased from 514,628 to 985,283 between the censuses of 1901 and 1981. However, from a peak of 311,645 in 1951 the population of the City of Nottingham has actually slumped to 268,257 (1981), making it just over 30,000 more than it was at the death of Queen Victoria. Nottingham is, of course, not alone in this trend, which has affected many of the largest urban areas in Britain in recent years. Inner residential districts have been cleared to make way for offices and shops, whilst many middle class inhabitants have moved out to villages within easy driving distance of their places of employment.

Of the larger towns in Nottinghamshire two have had startling increases in population during the first eight decades of the 20th century. East Retford has expanded from 3,436 in 1901 to 19,308 by 1981, whilst West Bridgford over the same time has gone up from 7,018 to 27,991. Nevertheless the three greatest urban centres outside the county town in 1901 still held their rank positions in 1981: Mansfield (from 21,445 to 59,015), Sutton-in-Ashfield combined with Hucknall Huthwaite (from 18,943 to 40,653), and Worksop (from 16,112 to 36,520). Ancient Newark on the other hand has sunk during the century down from sixth place in 1901 with 14,992 to ninth position with 24,016 in 1981. The only new town to emerge during this century has been Ollerton, which began with only 690 inhabitants to rise to 7,362 by 1981, outstripping Tuxford (2,547), Bingham (6,136) and Southwell (6,283). In Ollerton's case this was caused by the arrival and rapid growth of the coal mining industry, as will be seen below.

Increased urban population made it necessary to develop a public road transport system. The horse tram was to be found only in Nottingham, where the Nottingham & District Tramways Company had begun a service between St Paul's church and Trent Bridge on 17 September 1878. This was gradually extended to other roads, and in 1897 Nottingham City Council decided to take up the 21-year option clause and purchase the system. It was electrified as a result of this change in management, and the first new cars ran on New Year's Day, 1901. These were replaced in their turn by trolleybuses (from 10 April

Statue of First World War air ace, Capt. Albert Ball, Nottingham Castle

'Knife board' horse-bus on the Basford-Bulwell route in Nottingham

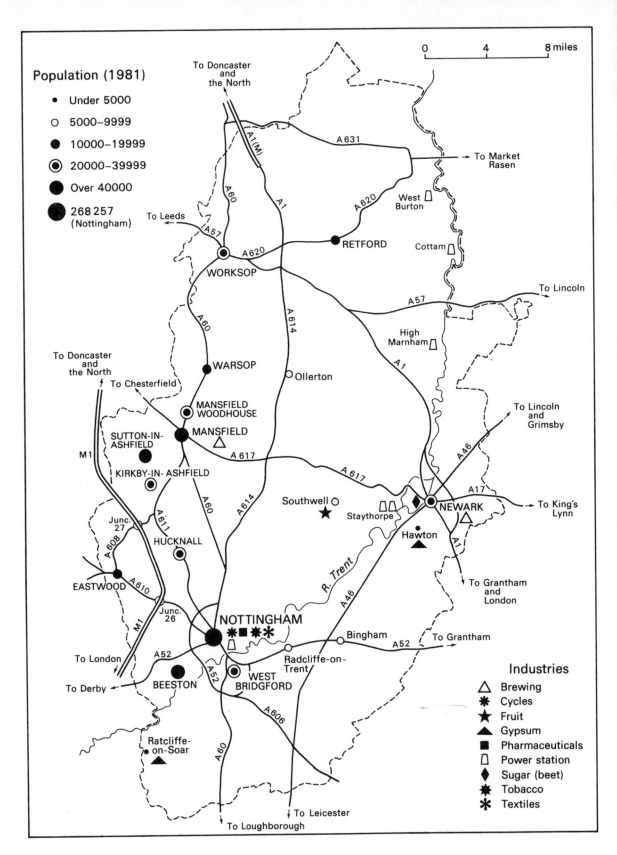

Population (1981)

- • Under 5000
- ○ 5000–9999
- ● 10000–19999
- ◉ 20000–39999
- ● Over 40000
- ● 268 257 (Nottingham)

To Doncaster and the North

0   4   8 miles

A1(M)

A631

To Market Rasen

A60

A1

A620

West Burton

Cottam

To Leeds

A57

A620

RETFORD

To Lincoln

WORKSOP

A57

A60

A614

High Marnham

To Doncaster and the North

WARSOP

Ollerton

A1

To Chesterfield

MANSFIELD WOODHOUSE

M1

SUTTON-IN-ASHFIELD

MANSFIELD

A617

To Lincoln and Grimsby

KIRKBY-IN-ASHFIELD

A46

A617

Junc. 27

A608

A611

A60

A614

Southwell ○

Staythorpe

NEWARK

A17

To King's Lynn

HUCKNALL

Hawton

To Grantham and London

EASTWOOD

A610

M1

R. Trent

A46

A1

NOTTINGHAM

Bingham

To Grantham

Junc. 26

To London

A52

Radcliffe-on-Trent

A52

To Derby

BEESTON

A52

WEST BRIDGFORD

A606

A60

Ratcliffe-on-Soar

Industries

- △ Brewing
- ✳ Cycles
- ★ Fruit
- ▲ Gypsum
- ■ Pharmaceuticals
- ⬠ Power station
- ◆ Sugar (beet)
- ✳ Tobacco
- ✱ Textiles

To Leicester

To Loughborough

Map 13. Twentieth-Century Nottinghamshire.

1927 between King Street and Basford) and also by motorbuses, which the municipal authorities had been introducing since 1920. The last tram ran in Nottingham on 5 September 1936. The trolleybuses themselves were finally ousted by the ubiquitous diesel bus on 30 June 1966. The Mansfield & District Light Railway Company began to operate their electric trams on 11 July 1905, and were acquired by the Mansfield District Tramways Ltd. the following year. This mode of public transport continued in Mansfield until 1932, when the trams were displaced by motorbuses.

More unusual was the Nottinghamshire & Derbyshire Tramways Company of 1903, immortalised in D. H. Lawrence's short story *Tickets Please*, set in the First World War when 'clippies' were employed on this inter-urban route. By 1913 this had linked Ripley in Derbyshire with Nottingham. On 5 October 1933 the electric trams were replaced by single-decked A.E.C. trolleybuses, which in their turn were withdrawn in favour of diesel buses from 25 April 1953.

Horse-drawn carriers' carts had plied between villages and their nearest market towns on market days from the middle of the 19th century until after the First World War. However, from 1919 onwards many of these operators and other ex-servicemen invested their savings in purchasing either Army and R.A.F. surplus vehicles or the new Model 'T' Ford chassis to replace the horse-drawn services and to establish new ones. One example was Elston miller W. W. Gash, who had been running a carrier's cart into Newark every Wednesday and Saturday, and substituted for this a Model 'T' in 1922. He paid the local carpenter to construct a large box containing 16 seats which could be affixed to the flat platform of the Ford which was used as a lorry on other weekdays. In 1932 Gash began to operate between Newark and Nottingham, the first of a new network of routes that he built up and which his firm still run. Of the larger bus operators to emerge between the Wars both East Midland Motor Services and Trent Traction owe their origins to railway company involvement, for the latter needed feeder routes to their main stations. For example, the L.M.S.R. made an agreement with the Mansfield & District Omnibus Company on 1 August 1929 for the partial financing of a new route between Mansfield and Newark, via Southwell. The railway company would pay for two of the vehicles working this service. This arrangement lasted until 13 June 1934. There were similar agreements to provide bus communications between Retford and Lincoln, and between Retford and Ollerton. In 1980 the Lincolnshire Road Car Company (which has a depot in Newark) combined with East Midland Motor Services to provide a through, stage-carriage route between Lincoln and Manchester, via Newark and Mansfield, given the

A.A. sign, Langar

113

title 'Lincman'. Unfortunately route X67 became an early victim of the deregulation of bus services, and ceased to operate after 25 October 1986.

The coal mining industry had gradually been expanding in an easterly direction as the growth of Ollerton demonstrates. However it was not until after the First World War that the first deep mines were sunk in the Bunter sandstone instead of in the more westerly Permo-Trias. Then after 1945 the first modern colliery was established on the eastern side of the Trent valley at Cotgrave.

.Not only has Nottinghamshire's mining industry been modernised with the sinking of such pits as Bevercotes, but twice this century a considerable percentage of the local work force has rebelled against their national union and gone its own way. During the 1926 lock-out which followed the General Strike, membership of the Nottinghamshire Miners' Association (affiliated to the Miners Federation of Great Britain) shrank as men began to drift back to work. With a total of only 500 underground in the county's pits at the end of July, this rose to 8,000 by the end of August, and on to 17,000 by the end of September. Many of them joined the new Nottinghamshire Miners' Industrial Union led by George Alfred Spencer (1872-1957), who was a local preacher, a checkweighman and Labour M.P. for the Broxtowe division from 1918 until 1929. His new union became the only one recognised by the Nottingham and Erewash Valley Colliery Owners' Association. However by 1935 the N.M.A.'s fortunes were beginning to improve, along with a rise in coal output from the East Midlands field. The crunch came with the Harworth Colliery dispute in which the N.M.I.U. had been unable to negotiate a favourable agreement over deductions from pay for dirt loaded with the coal onto the underground trams. Miners turned back to the N.M.A., which led to a withdrawal of labour from that pit in the autumn. The result of this industrial action was the merger of the rival unions to become the Nottinghamshire Miners' Federated Union on 1 September 1937 with G. A. Spencer as its President. Finally the loosely-knit M.F.G.B. was displaced by a unitary National Union of Miners on New Year's Day, 1945.

The bitterness caused by Spencerism was mirrored during the N.U.M.'s national strike of 1984/5 when, in spite of frequent visits by flying pickets from Yorkshire, the Nottinghamshire membership voted in a secret ballot by 20,188 to 7,285 on 15/16 March 1984 not to join this strike against pit closures. Even many of those who had voted in favour of militancy continued to work, albeit in an atmosphere of great bitterness. Eventually after a long and acrimonious dispute, on 6 June 1985 it was decided to break away and found the Union of Democratic

Mineworkers, supported by colleagues in Leicestershire and County Durham.

The coal mining industry is so important in the county because, since the Second World War, the River Trent has become lined with coal-burning power stations. Nottingham's own electricity works were opened officially on 17 September 1925, but the station on the banks of the river near the Wilford bridge was demolished in 1985. The Central Electricity Generating Board, set up after the industry had been nationalised by Attlee's Labour Government, brought into production stations at Staythorpe ('A' in 1950 and 'B' in 1962), High Marnham (1962), West Burton (1969) and Cottam (commissioned 1969).

In the 20th century another source of fuel has been discovered in the county, albeit on a much smaller scale. Oil occurs in certain places at depths between 3,000 feet and 4,000 feet in the Carboniferous rocks, which lie beneath the Trias and Mesozoic strata. Some of these reservoirs have been tapped, as at Eakring, Egmanton, Kelham Hills and across the Trent from Gainsborough, where 'nodding donkey' engines can be seen in action.

Gypsum excavation has continued both in the south-western corner of the county and also near Hawton (by Newark). Until gypsum deposits began to be worked in County Durham in 1922 no less than 40 per cent of the national output of this raw material came from the Hawton area. The gypsum is either mined or quarried. In 1907 while 101,147 tons were obtained by mining, quarrying accounted for only 27,382 tons. In this century additional uses have been found for this mineral rock, such as for garden rockeries. In its ground-up form of 'terra alba' or 'mineral white' it can be employed in bleaching and in the manufacture of paper, paint, oil and grease, as well as acting as a chemical manure.

Whereas the coming of the railways and the eclipse of the stage and Royal Mail coaches had tended to harm these communities which lay along the Great North Road, the advent in the 20th century of the motor car, the motor coach and the long distance lorry have brought new life to these same places – at least until they have been by-passed! Petrol filling stations and transport cafés have been built beside trunk routes like the A1 and A52. Thus very early road transport links between, for example, Newark and London have been restored. On the other hand, of the extensive network of motorways constructed since 1958, only a small section of the M1 between junctions 25 and 28 is actually within Nottinghamshire, and even the new M42, which will enable Nottingham drivers to by-pass Birmingham en route to the south-west, will stop 18 miles short of the county boundary when it opens in 1987.

Since the Second World War railway branch lines and wayside halts

115

The clock tower of Nottingham's Midland Railway Station

have tended to fade away, although Nottinghamshire as a whole has not suffered as much as more rural counties like Lincolnshire. In Nottingham the system has been rationalised with all train arrivals and departures concentrated at the old Midland Station, resulting in the closure of both Arkwright Street and the Victoria. The latter is the site of a vast shopping complex, though the clock tower has been retained. Some towns such as Southwell and Mansfield have been severed completely from the rail network; Mansfield is in the unenviable position of becoming the largest urban centre in England without its own station. However, as compensation, a new station called Mansfield Parkway has been opened on an existing line some miles away and is connected with the town by a bus link. Electrification is not due to reach the county before 1989, when the east coast main line between Peterborough and Leeds, via Newark and Retford, is scheduled to change over from HST 125s to electric locomotives. Nevertheless the introduction of these fast diesels in the early 1980s has reduced travelling time between Newark and Kings Cross to only one hour and forty minutes. In 1986 a new generation of diesel multiple units known as 'Sprinters' was introduced onto local services between Nottingham and Derby, Grantham and Lincoln. In addition considerable quantities of coal continue to be transported by rail, especially to the line of power stations along the banks of the Trent.

In 1918 the parliamentary constituencies of Nottinghamshire were reorganised with the creation of a fifth county seat called Broxtowe (after the Danish wapentake of that name). This immediately became a Labour stronghold, covering as it did much of the long-established coal mining area of the county. Apart from 1922/3 when the Liberals held the seat, Mansfield too became a safe Labour seat. On the other hand, between the wars, Newark and Rushcliffe remained staunchly Conservative. Bassetlaw changed its allegiance from Conservative to Labour in 1929. After the Second World War there was further change in constituency boundaries with the creation of new seats called Ashfield (won by Labour) and Carlton (won by Conservatives). In 1945 Newark was won by Labour, who retained it at successive general elections until the Tories regained it in their resurgence in 1979. On 28 April 1977 there was held one of the most sensational of all 20th-century by-elections, when the Conservative candidate (T. J. Smith) overturned a huge Labour majority of 22,915, converting it into a tiny Tory one of 264. Two years later, in the next general election, Labour retook the seat of Ashfield with a majority of 7,797. That by-election had been held because of the appointment of the sitting Labour member (David Marquand) to a post with the Common Market Commission. On 7 June 1979 was held the first direct election to the European Parliament, and the Labour

116

candidate (Michael Gallagher) won the Nottinghamshire Euroseat with a slim majority of 1,551, demonstrating the evenly-balanced position between the two main political parties at that date in the county. However in 1984 the Bassetlaw and Newark Westminster constituencies were added to the existing Lincolnshire Euroconstituency, which was retained by Conservative Bill Newton Dunn. In 1983 there were further redrawings of constituency boundaries, and only Rushcliffe remained unchanged. Two new seats were created – Gedling and Sherwood, both won by the Conservatives. The Alliance candidates' share of the votes cast varied from 16.7 per cent in Joe Ashton's Bassetlaw seat to 26.8 per cent in Ashfield. Alliance candidates came second only in Broxtowe, Gedling and Rushcliffe out of 11 Nottinghamshire seats; this compares with the S.D.P./Liberal candidates coming second in five of the six Lincolnshire constituencies.

Unlike some other counties (e.g. Yorkshire) Local Government boundaries were not changed in 1974 as far as the historical county was concerned. However, of course, the former rural district and urban district councils were replaced by new and enlarged district councils, thus ending the life of such civic authorities as Arnold U.D.C., Eastwood U.D.C., Hucknall Torkard U.D.C. and Warsop U.D.C., all set up in 1889.

Between 1901 and 1939 arable land in the county was drastically reduced from 240,000 acres to 145,266 acres. This largely reflected the area under cereals. In 1882 this amounted to 135,000 acres, but by 1889 it had already fallen by 20,000 acres, whilst 50 years later it was further reduced to 87,259 acres of grain crops. By 1939 wheat had become by far the most popular cereal crop (48,522 acres), in part due to a government subsidy in 1932 which added 10,000 acres of it in Nottinghamshire; much of it was grown in the Lower Trent valley. Oats (28,732 acres) now took second place, principally cultivated on the Forest Sand and Permian fringe of the county to provide food for sheep. Barley (8,636 acres in 1939) came a poor third, whereas back in 1880 it had covered as much ground as wheat 60 years later. Barley was now concentrated mainly around Bingham and Newark (still the centre of the brewing industry). Rye, at under 1,000 acres in 1939, was grown for thatching straw and for sheep fodder.

A new crop in the county was sugar beet, of which 7,882 acres were grown in 1939. This did particularly well on soils that were rich in lime. At its peak between the wars 12,000 acres of beet were under cultivation. Most of this harvest went to Kelham and Colwick sugar beet factories, opened in 1921 and 1924 respectively. However some beet farmers at the northern end of the county dispatched their crops either to Brigg or

Bardney in Lincolnshire. In 1974 the Kelham factory (by then renamed Newark) was expanded and modernised at a cost of £25,000,000. It now employs up to 475 workers during its peak production period of up to 140 days, when it processes 24 hours a day. The four concrete silos have a capacity of 12,000 tonnes of sugar, made from an average of 7,000 tonnes of beet a day. The total annual crop dealt with at Newark can be as high as 800,000 tonnes. As well as packaging Silver Spoon sugars in units of one kilogramme, molassed sugar beet pellets for animal food and up to 60,000 tonnes of spent lime are saleable by-products.

Field potatoes (first grown near Nottingham in the early 18th century by Robert Purcell, nicknamed 'Potato Robin') were cultivated chiefly in the Trent Valley's deep loam. In 1929, 7,577 acres were sown in the county. The comparatively low annual rainfall experienced in Nottinghamshire has aided their growth. Turnips, swedes and mangolds accounted for 14,427 acres in 1939, much of it on the Forest Sand and the Permian fringe. One thousand six hundred acres of cabbages were also grown at this time. Beans have a long history locally (e.g., the village name Barton-in-Fabis means Barton amongst the beans) and these continued to be cultivated on the Keuper Marl, whereas peas were grown in lighter soils.

For grazing and hay production 33,000 acres of clover were being grown on the eve of the Second World War. The two chief varieties were Common Dutch White and Red. Clover was grown throughout the county. There were also smaller areas of kohlrabi, lucerne, mustard, rape and vetches. On the market gardening side carrots, celery, onions and rhubarb were all cultivated, especially around Nottingham and in the Greet valley near Southwell.

Fruit, and in particular the Bramley Seedling apple, was also associated with the cathedral town. This had originally been marketed in 1837 by a local grower, Matthew Bramley, whose niece, Mary Brailsford, had grown the first such tree from a pip planted in 1815. Orchards were scattered all along the Trent and, until the branch railway lines and their accompanying goods yards fell victim to Dr. Beeching's axe, fruit was loaded at night onto rail wagons ready for dispatch next day. Crops raised included black currants, damson, gooseberries, plums, raspberries and strawberries. Rose trees were grown at Chilwell, Mapperley and Ruddington.

The 20th century has seen the planting of many saplings by the Forestry Commission (founded in 1919) and other interested parties, so that in the 15 years between 1924 and 1939 the county's woodlands increased from 30,253 acres to 42,566 – a process that has continued in later decades. Much of the new planting was of Scots firs and other

Bramley apple

118

coniferous species, giving Nottinghamshire a greater acreage of trees than any other East Midlands county.

Turning to livestock, by 1939 cattle had more than made up for their decline during the Agricultural Depression, almost reaching 100,000 head in the final quarter of the 19th century. The accent was now on dairy farming, and this was particularly true in the southern half of the county. Milk was supplied not only to the city of Nottingham, but also to Leicester and London. A soft cheese recipe for Colwick cheese continued to be employed, and Stilton was produced at Colston Bassett, Langar and Willoughby-on-the-Wolds. By 1939 the Milk Marketing Board had arrangements with 345 farms in Nottinghamshire, whilst Nottingham Dairy Ltd. was supplied by another 34 farms in the county.

On the other hand sheep flocks continued to decline; the aggregate of animals grazing in the county dwindled to 142,857 by 1939. Many were to be found on the Forest Sand and on the carrs (drained fenland) at the northern extremity of the county. Suffolks replaced Lincolnshire Longwools for crossbreeding with the indigenous Forest sheep.

Pigs doubled in numbers to 50,000 swine by 1939, including 6,000 breeding sows, mostly of the Middle White breed. Poultry farms were on the increase in the first four decades of the century, rearing 780,000 birds by 1939, the vast majority of which were chicken.

The last quarter of the 20th century has seen a concerted effort by Nottinghamshire County Council to promote tourism. They have erected distinctive brown and cream directional signs to various attractions within the county, and have co-ordinated public transport, based on the new Visitors Centre near the famous Major Oak in Sherwood Forest. From this focal point tourists are ferried in buses (including specially-painted open toppers) owned by half a dozen operators to such places as Clumber Park (once the home of the Dukes of Newcastle), the Lound National Mining Museum, Newstead Abbey (home of Lord Byron), North Leverton windmill, Papplewick pumping station, Pets Corner at Treswell and the Winthorpe Air Museum (outside Newark). The Robin Hood Way is an 88-mile public footpath that stretches from Edwinstow church to Nottingham castle. Then there are the Attenborough Nature Reserve, Centre Parc, Rufford (Dutch-financed and organised holiday centre) and the Holme Pierrepont National Water Sports Centre, near West Bridgford, where the 1986 World Rowing Championships were held, bringing Britain its first two gold medals.

As we have seen in this volume, Nottinghamshire has often advanced in a different direction from the other East Midlands counties. When there has been revolt against the Crown it has remained loyal to its sovereign. Yet it has been far from docile and conformist. The Luddites were more active in Nottinghamshire than in any of the four counties in which their riots occurred. Twice in this century the miners of the county have broken away from their national organisation and formed their own body.

Neither has Nottinghamshire shared the same industries as its neighbours, developing its own such as alabaster, stockings, lace, tobacco and pharmaceuticals. Again, the heavy engineering industry that has provided the *raison d'être* for Derby, Gainsborough and Lincoln to remain important centres after 1850 is not to be found in Nottinghamshire, apart, perhaps, from the cycle industry in Nottingham itself. Although many people automatically think of Burton-on-Trent when brewing is mentioned, Newark and Mansfield have rivalled that Staffordshire town in their time. This particular industry requires large quantities of barley and, although Nottinghamshire is not in the same league agriculturally as its close neighbour Lincolnshire, nevertheless farming did and still does play a vital role in the county's economy.

Politically Nottinghamshire in this century has not been classed as either heartland Conservative or Labour territory in the same way as Surrey or County Durham. Nottingham city itself in the 1980s is regarded by political commentators as a barometer as to how England as a whole might vote in a general election.

We began with the River Trent and we must end with it. When Jesse Boot, on being elevated to a barony, adopted its name as his title, he was reflecting its importance in the development of his native county. Not only geographically has this long and vital waterway determined the economy of Nottinghamshire (from the carriage on it of raw materials of yesteryear to the still expanding power station network of today), but it also serves as a political boundary between North and South, as well as the deciding factor in how Newark and Nottingham remain consistently the two principal towns in the shire. However, since the coming of first the railway and later of the internal combustion engine, Mansfield and to a lesser extent Retford and Worksop, along with the urban sprawl on the edge of Sherwood Forest in the coal measures, have rivalled the stature of these two long-established towns. A yet later development has been the growth of small market towns into commuter satellite towns as has happened in the past 20 years with Bingham, a phenomenon which is taking place elsewhere in the Britain of the 1980s.

War memorial, Nottingham

Bibliography

Anglo-Saxon Chronicle.

Barley, Maurice, *Nottinghamshire Medieval Studies*, 1959.

Bates, Alan, *Directory of Stage Coach Services, 1836*, 1969.

Beresford, Maurice and Hurst, John, *Deserted Medieval Villages*, 1971.

Boots the Chemists, *100 Years of Shopping at Boots*, 1977.

Brown, Cornelius, *A History of Newark*, 1904.

Chaffers, William, *Marks and Monograms on Pottery and Porcelain*, 1963.

Creswell Crags pamphlet.

Cummins, John, *Railway Motorbuses and Bus Services in the British Isles*, 1978.

Dalling, Philip, *Erewash Valley Portrait*, 1980.

Defoe, Daniel, *A Tour Through England and Wales* (Letter VIII).

East Midlands Archaeology Reports.

Edwards, K. C., *The Land of Britain: Part 60 – Nottinghamshire*, 1944.

English Place-Names Society, Nottinghamshire volume.

Fox, Malcolm, *Newark in the Civil War*, 1985.

Frere, S. S., *Britannia*, 1966.

Gay, Dr. John, *The Geography of Religion in England*, 1971.

Griffin, Alan R., *The Miners of Nottinghamshire, 1914-1944*, 1962.

Griffin, Alan R., *County Under Siege – Nottinghamshire in the Miners' Strike, 1984-85*, 1985.

Hadfield, Charles, *The Canals of the East Midlands*, 1966.

Holt, J. C., *Robin Hood*, 1982.

Iliff, R. and Bayvolley, W., *Victorian Nottingham: A Story in Pictures*.

Leleux, R., *Regional History of Railways: East Midlands*, 1983.

Martin-Jenkins, C., *Wisden Book of County Cricket*, 1981.

Mitchell, Jean, *Great Britain, Geographical Essays*, 1962.

Morris, J. (ed.), *Domesday Book: Nottinghamshire*, 1977.

Ormsbee, T. H., *English China and its Marks*, 1959.

Pevsner, Nikolaus, *The Buildings of England: Nottinghamshire*, 1951.

Philpotts, R., *The Grantham Canal – Early Days*, 1976.

Pigott, Stanley, *Hollins – A Study of Industry*, 1965.

Renn, Derek, *Norman Castles in Britain*, 1968.

Roberts, Ian F., *Nottingham Castle*, 1985.

Smurthwaite, David, *The Ordnance Survey Complete Guide to the Battlefields of Britain.*

Summers, Norman, *A Prospect of Southwell*, 1974.

Thorold, H., *The Shell Guide to Nottinghamshire*, 1984.

Thoroton Society Proceedings.

Todd, Malcolm, *Coritani*, 1975.

Victoria County History of Nottinghamshire.

Wacher, John, *The Towns of Roman Britain*, 1974.

Weir, Christopher, *A Prospect of Nottinghamshire*, 1986.

John Wesley's Journal.

Witton, A. M., *Buses of the East Midlands*, 1983.

Wood, A. C., *A History of Nottinghamshire*, 1947.

Wood, A. C., *A History of University College, Nottingham, 1881-1948*, 1948.

Wyncoll, Peter, *The Nottingham Labour Movement*, 1985.

Nottingham University

Index

Farnsfield, 19, 28
Felley, 55, 60
Fenton, 34, 104
Ferrers: Henry, Earl of Derby, 37; William, Earl of Derby, 44
Fiennes, Celia, 71, 92
Finningley, 34
Fiskerton, 52, 73
Fleming, Alan, 48
Flemmaugh, Thomas de, 55
Fossdyke, 24
Fosse Way, 21, 29, 46, 52
Fox: George, 76; Samuel, 99
Fran, 34
Frost, Robert, 73

Gainsborough, 75, 82, 86, 108, 115, 120
Gallacher, Michael, 117
Gamston, 73, 76
Garton, Thomas, 74
Gash, W. W., 113
Gedling (constituency), 117
George V, King, 100
Gilbert of Ghent, 36, 54
Gladstone, W. E., 100, 109
Gloucester, Robert, Earl of, 44
Glover, Edward, 98
Godekin of Revel, 49
Godiva (Godgifu), Lady, 31
Godwin the priest, 34
Gonalston, 34, 58
Gotham, 17, 28, 29, 34, 72, 99
Grantham: 80, 81, 85, 86, 116; Canal, 84
Greasley, 55, 75, 82, 84, 104
Green, Henry & Co., 94
Greet, River, 118
Grey, John de, 44
Grim, 34
Gringley-on-the-Hill, 14, 36
Gunn, George, 102
Gunthorpe, 17, 94
Gunthorpe, Thomas, 78
Guthrum, 29
Gylbert, William, 62
Gylham, William, 60

Hacker, Col. Francis, 68
Hadlee, Richard, 102
Hall, William, 78
Halloughton Dumble, 14
Harby, 57
Hardstaff, Joseph, jnr., 101
Hargreaves, James, 73
Harold II, King, 36
Harworth, 78, 114
Hasna, 46
Hatfield Chase, battle of, 26
Haughton, 75
Haunsley, Ralph, 55
Hawksworth, 28, 35

Hawton, 14, 34, 115
Hazelford, 94
Headon, 28, 75
Heanor, 81
Heath, Prior Nicholas, 60
Hedderley, Daniel, 72
Hedworth, Ralph, 59
Helwys, Thomas, 75
Hemlock Stone, 13
Henderson, Sir John, 65
Hendred, Bishop Joseph, 110
Henrietta Maria, Queen, 65
Henry: I, 46, 47; II, 35, 38, 44-6, 50, 55, 58; III, 44, 46; IV, 57; VI, 51, 90; VII, 52, 53, 57; VIII, 54, 60, 62
Heriz, William de, 58
High Marnham, 115
Hobhouse, Sir John, 100
Hockerton, 34
Hockley, 73
Hodstock, 34
Holles: Denzil, 63; Sir John, 63
Hollins family, 106
Holme, 28, 94
Holme Pierrepont, 14, 17, 19, 28, 36, 72, 82, 119
Hood, Robin, 39, 40, 44, 99
Hooton, Elizabeth, 76
Hoveringham, 14, 17, 72
Hucknall Huthwaite, 103, 111
Hucknall Torkard, 74, 98, 103, 117
Hudson, George, 85
Hugh, Earl, 36
Humber, Thomas, 97, 98
Hutchinson: George, 64, 65; John, 64, 67, 68

Idle, River, 14, 25, 48, 57, 61
Ilkeston, 81
Illingworth, Sir Richard, 51
Immingham, 75
Ingham (lace maker), 73
Ireton, Col. Henry, 65, 68
Isabella, Queen, 45, 57

James: I, 53, 63, 75; II, 64, 91
Jessop, William, 82
John, King, 46, 47
Johnson, Rev. John, 59

Kegworth, 108
Kelham, 29, 115, 117
Kendall, Samuel, 76
Keyser family, 49
Keyworth, 34
Kilby, William, 74
Kimberley, 70
Kingston, dukes of, 65, 77
Kingston-on-Soar, 28, 34, 36
Kirkby-in-Ashfield, 41, 98, 103
Kirton, 34
Kneesall, 28